Rebirth
POSSESSING THE PROMISE

ASHLEY HICKS

ISBN 979-8-9870123-2-1 (Paperback)

Scriptures marked NIV are taken from the NEW INTERNATIONAL VERSION (NIV): Scripture taken from THE HOLY BIBLE, NEW INTERNATIONAL VERSION ®. Copyright© 1973, 1978, 1984, 2011 by Biblica, Inc.™. Used by permission of Zondervan

Scriptures marked KJV are taken from the KING JAMES VERSION (KJV): KING JAMES VERSION, public domain.

Published and designed by Ministry Event Marketing

Printed in the United States of America

DEDICATION

To my incredible children, Tiyrel, Tiyler, Tiyrah, Tory, Trenton, Trevian, and Tameer,

I want you to know how deeply I love and appreciate each one of you. Thank you for sticking with me as I learned to be a mom while raising you. Your unwavering faith in me has been my greatest strength and motivation. In your eyes, I have always been a superhero, and that belief has carried me through the toughest times. You are the reason I have made it this far, and I am so proud of the amazing individuals you are becoming. I love you all more than words can express, and I am forever grateful for your love and support.

With all my love, Mom

To the Love of my Life, Tonshad,

Your love has illuminated my life in ways I never thought possible. Your patience, understanding, and unwavering support have given me strength and courage beyond measure. You see me for who I truly am, embracing my past with compassion and loving me unconditionally. Your presence in our family with our children and in our future together is invaluable.

Every day, your dedication and genuine love inspire me. I am endlessly grateful for how you cherish and uplift me I Will forever be honored to be your wife. This book is dedicated to you, with all my love and appreciation for the remarkable man you are.

With all my heart,

Your Wife Ashley

CONTENTS

INTRODUCTION

Welcome to *Rebirth Vol. 2: Possessing the Promise.*

In this continuation of my journey, we delve deeper into the process of healing from the traumas of both childhood and adulthood. Healing is an ongoing, ever-evolving process—it's not a one-size-fits-all solution. Each of us experiences and processes our pain differently, and that's perfectly okay.

As you turn these pages, I invite you to walk with me through the ups and downs, the victories and setbacks. This book is not just a recounting of my experiences, but a guide and a companion for your own healing journey. Remember, healing takes time. Be patient with yourself. Love yourself. Learn to give yourself the grace you so freely extend to others.

You've already taken the brave step of seeking to heal, and for that, I commend you. Know that you are not alone in this journey. Together, we can embrace the promise of a brighter, healthier future.

You've got this!

Coach Ashley Hicks

CHAPTER 14: MOTHERHOOD

Hey Sis,

Are you still with me on this incredible journey? I sure hope so because the story of my transformation has been nothing short of amazing! Having you along for the ride has made it even more special. I've come to realize that sometimes it takes one queen to help another unlock her divine purpose and unleash the superpowers that God has placed within her. No worries, Sistah! I've got your back because we're in this together!

So, let's dive right in. The last time we talked, I had just found out I was pregnant and shared the news with my son's father. Stay tuned as I reveal what happened next and how it shaped me into the woman I am today.

Tony and I pulled up to a nearby Long John Silver's—it was just five minutes from the school. As we caught up, I felt that old spark rekindle. He still looked the same but was dressed nicely today in blue denim jeans, a button-up orange polo shirt, and, to my surprise, a dark brown belt.

As we talked, I realized some things never change. Tony still had this habit of randomly staring at me without saying a word, especially when I asked him questions. It was like he was stuck on a pop quiz, and I'd have to snap him out of it with a "hello."

I think Tony believed he was answering me, but the words stayed trapped in his head. Despite this, lunch was enjoyable, and before we parted ways, Tony asked me to keep him updated about the baby and to let me know if I needed

He dropped me back at school, and I headed off to class.

Once I stopped hiding my pregnancy and everyone at school knew, I felt so much more comfortable. Sure, sometimes I felt embarrassed, but mostly, I just didn't care. There were days when adults were rude and offered unwanted advice, but overall, I got a lot of attention, both good and bad.

My friends and others often wanted to rub my belly, help me with things, and, of course, bring me food! I kind of liked these perks. They'd even offer to carry my books. I got to skip out on P.E. activities except for basic walking, which was fantastic. I loved being pregnant; it gave me an excuse to be lazy

3

without anyone actually calling me lazy.

I wasn't the only pregnant girl at my high school; there was another girl, same age and race, with a due date just two weeks apart from mine. Honestly, it felt pretty good to have someone like me at the same school. I was definitely an oddball, waddling down the halls with what felt like a basketball in my belly.

The next day, I had my first doctor's appointment with Dr. Alyssa Ta, an obstetrician-gynecologist. Her office was in a medical building across from the University Community Hospital on Fletcher Ave and Bruce B. Downs Blvd in Tampa, FL.

My mom and I walked into the lobby, and she checked me in with the front desk receptionist before we took a seat. My mom handled all the paperwork, presented her insurance card and ID, and soon we were called to the back.

The nurse led us to the first of three medical rooms. The walls were painted tan, and a burgundy medical bed with a strip of paper sat in the center. In the corner was a burgundy chair with tan legs, and a long counter filled with medical devices and containers of bandages, Q-tips, and other items lined one wall.

Shortly after, a beautiful, short Chinese woman with free-flowing hair walked in. She had a contagious smile, flawless skin, and eyes shaped like slanted pecans. Her presence filled the room with a soothing, warm feeling.

She had a clipboard in her hand and began to introduce herself to the two of us.

"Hello, My name is Dr. Alyssa Ta. How are you today?" she asked.

"I'm doing well," I said, smiling back at her.

"Hello, Mom, hope your day is going great," Dr. Ta said, turning to my mom.

"I've had better days. Given the circumstances, I'm not so happy," my mom replied.

"Yes, I understand. I'm here to support you. Let's go ahead and get started. I'll ask you some questions, and we can go from there," Dr. Ta said.

After completing the initial medical questionnaire, it was time for my ultrasound. This imaging test would examine the baby, check its size, height, and weight, and reveal the baby's sex. It was an exciting moment, as we were about to get a first glimpse of the little one growing inside me.

Dr. Ta asked me to lie back, then rolled in a machine with a black-and-white screen and a handheld device connected to it. She placed some cold blue gel on the device and began to rub it across my belly. As soon as it touched my stomach, the baby moved, creating a wave-like motion. Dr. Ta jumped at the flutters and laughed.

She explained to my mom and me what we were looking at. The screen showed the baby in a profile position, and I could see all its limbs and even its brain.

"Are we going to be able to find out what it is?" I asked eagerly.

Before Dr. Ta could respond, my mom interrupted, "Well, we were just looking into getting rid of it, so that doesn't really matter."

"Well, Mrs. McCalla, I'm sorry, but we don't offer those types of services here in this office. Also, Ashley is about 28 weeks pregnant; she's too far along, and it would be quite traumatic," Dr. Alyssa Ta informed us.

"28 weeks?!! We just can't do this!" my mom screamed.

I just put my head down. Hearing someone say they wanted to get rid of the baby growing inside of me made me feel sick to my stomach.

However, Dr. Ta had a way of calming the mood. Her spirit was soothing, and I felt safe in her office. I was grateful she was standing up for me and basically saving my baby's life.

My mom's face was full of disappointment and anger. She made me feel awful, repeatedly calling me disgusting and saying I was a baby having a baby. I already knew I had messed up, but her words only made it worse.

Dr. Ta printed out the pictures from the ultrasound and gave me some literature about pregnancy at twenty-eight weeks. She also handed me a bag full of goodies, including prenatal vitamins, healthy snacks, pregnancy education books, and a T-shirt that read, "I have a bun in the oven." I giggled when I saw the shirt and placed it back in the bag.

My mom frowned at me and said, "Hurry up and get dressed so we can go."

"Are there any questions for me?" asked Dr. Ta.

"No, not at the moment," my mom replied. "Thank you."

I stood up and started to get dressed. As I removed my medical robe, my full body was exposed while I gathered my clothes from the chair in the corner. My stomach protruded prominently, resembling a swollen watermelon. At 5'3" and weighing about 111 lbs, I felt distinctly out of proportion.

As I pulled on my shirt, the baby began to move. I looked down at my stomach and saw it ripple in a wave-like motion. I gently rubbed my belly, feeling the baby respond to my touch.

Then, there was a knock at the door.

"Come in," my mom answered.

It was Dr. Ta. "Oh, I'm sorry. So, yes, we have the sex of the baby. Is now a good time?" she asked.

My mom remained silent and looked away. I eagerly said yes. I was anxious to know the baby's gender, though I secretly hoped for a boy. I believed a son would love me unconditionally, unlike others I had known.

Unable to contain myself any longer, I asked, "What is it, Dr. Ta?"

Dr. Ta walked over to me with a picture and pointed out a tiny figure in the ultrasound image.

"That, my dear, is a little baby boy!"You are having a boy! She raved with excitement! The more excited Dr.Ta was about this news, the more aggravated my mom became.

I didn't show any emotion or excitement. In fear of what my mom would think or say to me, I was having flashbacks of her hitting me when she found out the news of me being pregnant in the first place. I sat there with a neutral face, but inside, I was so happy I was having a boy.

"Thank you, Dr. Ta,"I said.

"You are most welcome. I know this is not the ideal time to have a baby, but babies are bundles of joy, and you will be fine."She came over and gave me a big hug! Surprisingly, that hug really made me feel better. It was like a security blanket over me. It made me feel I was actually going to be okay.

I was terrified for my future. I now had a son on the way, and I would be a real mom, too. My due date was March 25, 2004. It was the second week of February, so I still had a few more weeks until he was born.

At this point, I was fully dressed and ready to walk out. My mom grabbed her purse, and as we walked out the door, she began to mumble.

"That's a full-grown baby, twenty-eight weeks! You felt that baby moving!"She said

I didn't respond, If I didn't learn anything else during this situation, I learned to JUST BE QUIET! We both made it to the car parked outside. I sat in the backseat and started imagining how my son would look. I wanted to hurry and call Tony to let him know. I wondered if he was going to be happy. Then again, he already had two children at eighteen. I took a deep breath in and then breathed out. This wasn't what I wanted to happen. But hey, it was too late now.

From the front seat, I could hear my mom dialing someone's number. There was a male's voice on the other end. I hoped it wasn't Ernesto. Indeed it came out to be that it wasn't. It was my dad.

My mom called him to let him know I was pregnant and how far along I was. He was surprised, and he sounded shocked and upset. I sat there, not saying anything, but how could he be surprised or upset at me? This very man walked out on me years ago. He did not teach me anything and was never there to protect me. I was angry at him. My mom then turned around and said my dad was coming to my grandmother's to come to meet me in a few.

That was not something I was looking forward to. My dad was very inconsistent, and we didn't have a good relationship. I never felt that my dad truly loved me. I believed everything he did concerning me or my brother was just out of obligation or to prove something to my mom. The thing he didn't do for us was to get back at my mom, too. They didn't have a good co-parenting relationship at all, and they both failed me and my brother. Because in the end, we were the two who suffered from their immaturity.

Moments later, we pulled up to my grandmother's house. As we pulled into her driveway, I saw my dad's Green Cadillac parked at the end of the road. I stepped out with this shirt that was my brother's, but you could clearly see my stomach. It was no longer necessary to even try to hide it. My dad got out of the car and stood by the back of his car. My mom went into the house and left the two of us alone. I walked over to him.

"Hey Papa" I said to greet him.

"Hey girl, So you have a baby on the way., Huh?

Then he grabbed me and hugged me; I began to cry. He whispered it was going to be o.k and held me close. At that moment, him not being there for me no longer mattered. That moment is what mattered and what I needed. I wished he was more involved, but my dad was one-sided. It was either his way or the highway. The craziest thing was I had to fight for a relationship with him. No Daughter should ever have to fight for the attention & love of her father.

We stood out before my grandmother's house and talked for a while. Then, my dad had other obligations, so he told me goodbye before getting into the car and driving off. I stayed on the porch for a minute. I already knew my grandma would have a lot to say once inside. So, I was enjoying the peace while I was outside. I walked in to grab the cordless phone. This was probably a good time to tell Tony the news.

I walked into my grandmother's den. I'm glad no one was in there to greet me. I continued into the kitchen and grabbed the phone off the wall. I dialed Tony's cell phone number. He answered rather quickly.

"Hello"? He answered

"Hey, this Ashley,"I said while smiling. I couldn't believe I was having this boy's baby.

"Yeah, what's up with you "? he asked.

"Well, today I found out I'm having a boy."

"A boy, huh? Ok, what are you naming him?"

"I don't know just yet. I was thinking maybe it's Terrance or Tyrese.

He didn't seem intrigued by any name I suggested, but of course, you know, he didn't say a word.

I shifted the conversation because sitting in complete silence was pretty awkward.

"The doctor said that I am about 28 weeks, so I think I will have the baby between 38 and 40 weeks, so I have 10 or so weeks left,"I said.

"Yeah, that will be here before you know it, "He said

As I was going to say something else, My grandmother opened the front door to ask me something. Before Tony could hear her. I told him that I would call him back. Unfortunately, after that phone call, Tony & I wouldn't see each other again until I gave birth to my son.

Several Months Later, on March 15, 2004, I gave birth to my first child, Tiyrel. He was light-skinned,weighed about 6 lbs even, and was 21 inches long. He had a head full of curly hair, and his back was full of hair as well. It was so funny and weird because it was shaped in the letter T down his back as I held him against my chest. I fell in love with him right that second. I didn't know how to be a mother. However, from that point forward, I promised him I would always give him my all.

Bringing a newborn home was a little challenging, I found myself not getting any sleep, and I was often tired and moody. My entire life now just consisted of changing diapers, making bottles, and talking to a baby who never talked back to me. Tony wasn't at the hospital when I gave birth to Tiyrel. He went behind my back and told his mom he didn't think Tiyrel was his son. I was pretty hurt and didn't understand why he would say something like that.

Instead of being honest with me, he and his mom were sneaking, trying to pick Tiyrel up to go and get the test on my baby without me knowing. I remember Tony calling me asking to pick up Tiyrel when I was home alone. I called my mom to let her know, but she refused to let Tiyrel But go with Tony. I was so mad at her! Why wouldn't she let this man come pick up his son? At that moment, she didn't let me know, but later on, she did.

When my mom got home that evening, she said she wanted to be home when Tony came around, and she just felt that something in her spirit was not right with letting the baby go with his dad. Come to find out, she was right. My mom called Tony's mother and offered to come to get the baby now that she was home. His mother declined, stating it was too late to get him. My mom was a bit confused, being that it was only about 5:30 pm in the evening.

"I'm a little confused,"said my mother to Trish, Tony's mother.

9

"Well, Tony was picking up Tiyrel to do a DNA test on him, but the place is closed now."

"DNA Test?" If that was necessary, why didn't you guys just say that versus being sneaky? Asked my mother

Tony's mother didn't really have a response, and before my mom got even more aggravated than she was, she ended the call, but before doing so, she advised Trish they could make an appointment and we would be sure to be there.

A week later, The DNA appointment was scheduled at a medical facility on Florida Avenue in Tampa, FL. Tony was walking out as we were walking in. I didn't say a word to him; I walked past him like he didn't even exist. When I walked into the building, we were greeted by a short Spanish lady.

She introduced herself and asked for our names. She took us into a room and asked us to sit in a chair. She took out a long cotton swab, and she rubbed both sides of my cheeks and then the same for Tiyrel for just a few seconds. It was really quick, and it did not hurt at all.

The lady informed us that the test results would be available in about two days. They were going to call us and also mail the results. We walked out and went on about our day. I was anxious for the results to hurry up. All this time, Tony did nothing to help our son, and his reasoning was that he didn't know if my son was his. I couldn't wait until it was proven otherwise.

It was around the summertime again. We were in July. Tiyrel was around five months old at this time. My brother and I were away in St. Augustine with our summer school program. We were there visiting colleges and visited their campuses. The summer program paid us to come to the camp daily and learn new things! It was really fun. My brother had a cell phone. However, the area that we were in did not get any good signal at all. We couldn't dial out or even get any incoming calls.

Out of nowhere, my brother came from the front of the bus that we were on, and his phone started to ring. I was confused about how he was now able to get service! It was our mother. She was calling to give us the DNA test results. All of a sudden, I got really nervous, but it wasn't because I didn't know he was the father; it was because this whole process was not familiar to me. Seconds later, my brother called my name and passed my phone down the bus aisle so I could talk to my mother.

"Hello"? I said

"Hey Ash, I have the test results chy. The test is 99.99999999% Tony is the father,"She screamed.

"I knew it! And see his ugly butt come trying to be sneaky and waste that money on a test!

"Yes, girl, you were right. You did tell everybody you were sure. I was a little worried because Tiyrel came out looking closer to a Caucasian baby than anything.

We both laughed. I thanked my mother for the information and went to the back of the bus where my brother was. I let him in on the news. He said he already knew that. He said Tiyrel looked exactly like his dad. I finally was relieved. Hopefully, now that Tony knew my son was his, he would actually be a better father and a provider.

As time went on, fast-forward to Tiyrel being about a year old. There was no change in Tony's fatherly skills. He barely came around, was not active in his life, and barely gave me any money for Tiyrel. My son was the one suffering in the end. Nobody on his dad's side of the family ever cared for him or was in his life.

The good thing is, that I did have some helpful resources, there was a program called Title 20 or School Readiness. This program assisted single mothers and teen parents with subsidized daycare fees. So what would normally cost $125 a week for a baby? I had a parent fee of only $2.25 a day. There was also a program called WIC (Woman, Infants, Children) This program was designed to provide food, health care referrals, and nutrition education for low-income pregnant, breastfeeding, and non-breastfeeding postpartum women and to infants and children up to age 5 who are found to be at nutritional risk. They provided Healthy foods and about 10 cans of formula, free of charge to you.

Then the other perk was that my grandmother was a daycare provider, So ultimately, I didn't pay her anything. Well, until that is when she would get mad at me and calculate later what I owed her. I giggled to myself, thinking about this. My grandmother was the person that helped me the most out of anybody. She watched my baby while I was in school and sometimes while I worked. She bought him clothes, shoes, and book bags. Whatever Tiyrel needed, she got it! My mother had choir rehearsals a lot, so she rarely did unless I wanted to hang out. This was rare, though. I always had my baby with me. Sometimes, I had to fight with my mom even to be allowed to take my baby with me to places. My side of the family was the only support that I had, which was My mom, My grandaddy, Ernesto, and My brother. This was my immediate go-to for the both of us, my first year or so into motherhood.

Tony's Family was non-existent. Tiyrel was now a year old. I was sixteen years old. Time had really flown by fast. I was still in school, but during my freshman year, I played around a lot. I had started skipping school again. Especially since Tony ended up having his apartment next door to my high school, I would hang out with him all day and then go to school at the end of the day. I hoped I could convince him to be a better father to Tiyrel. I just felt school wasn't for me. I had to try very hard to pass my math classes. I did not enjoy that subject at all! I just wanted to hurry and be an adult already and get on with my life.

For some reason, my overall goal to finish school was to hurry and be an adult so that I could have a family. I wanted to create a family that I never had.

After getting picked up from school one afternoon, I finally made it home. I had to be at work (Quiznos Sandwich Shop)at 6:00 p.m., so I would have to wait for my mom to come home. My brother was heading off to work; he was working at a Winn Dixie grocery store. This left Me, Tiyrel, and Ernesto at home. My mother wasn't home from work yet.

I went to my room, put Tiyrel down to play with his toys, and turned on the Television for him in my room. Then I noticed our clothes were piling up in the corner. It was time for me to wash clothes. I'd better get to it, before my mother sees this and then starts going crazy.

I grabbed my hamper and put our clothes in the basket and headed to the laundry room. I began to start running the water in the washer machine and then put the washing powder in and then began to place my clothes in the washer machine to be washed. After I did that, I checked the dryer, and I saw it was full of towels that needed to be taken out. I grabbed another empty basket and bent over to get the towels from the dryer. As I was removing all of them, someone walked in from behind me. Pushing up against my butt and wrapping their arm around my waist. I jumped up and moved closer to the dryer.

"Omg,"I screamed as I looked back, and it was Ernesto. He proceeded to still press against me and draw me closer to him as I was facing him.

"Come on, come on, he said in this low, nasty-sounding voice."

"No, I screamed!"I dropped the clothes basket, pushed away from him, got around him, and ran straight to my room!

When I returned to my room, I slammed and locked the door behind me. Tiyrel was sitting on the floor playing with his trucks and watching Barney & Friends on T.V. I sat on the floor. I was in utter shock at what had just happened. Why was Ernesto Groping me!??? This was so nasty and weird. Tiyrel walked over to me and sat in my lap; he had no idea what was happening. I kissed him on his forehead. I did not dare go out of the room until my mother would come home.

Whenever that would be..........

Now, here I sat at sixteen, trying to process why my mother's husband was groping me. This was all out of line. What could I do??? Nothing, because I didn't matter. I just had to deal with this on my own. My mom, for sure, would not, believe me, she was too in love and caught up in her own life.

Chapter 15: "Yes, Again"

I was excited that it was now my senior year in high school. I was so ready for all this to be over with. However, because my mom had bought me a car when I was sixteen, I had more access to drive and leave school when I wanted. All the Skipping Classes or not going to school crept up on me. All the fooling around in 10th grade was no longer cute or funny.

I had a meeting with my guidance counselor, Mrs. Poole. She told me that I was missing a few credits and that if they were not met by May 1, 2004, then I was not going to walk with my class. I could not allow this to happen, so Mrs. Poole signed me up for night school at Tech High School right up the street from my school. I attended night school for a few months to complete the classes that I had previously failed.

I was in OJT ("on-the-job training"), So after the second period, we could go home or work. Whatever it was, we had to do it. I was working at Boston Market Restaurant at that time. My normal schedule wasn't until later that evening, but I left school anyway. They didn't know what I had going on. I worked at the location in Tampa on Fowler Ave. There were tons of food restaurants on this strip. It was conveniently located near the University Mall as well. We were in the middle of the local attractions. This was a hotspot. Across the street was a Taco Bell. I often walked across the street to grab some tacos because I would get tired of rotisserie chicken from my job.

One day, on my lunch, I went to Taco Bell to grab something. I walk up to the counter. A red-haired White girl takes my order and then walks away to prepare it. As I'm standing there playing on my phone. I see a tall dark chocolate gentleman, low cut fade, on the line making the food. He smiled at me, and then he kept staring at me every chance he got. I would look off every now and again but would soon catch him looking at me right in my eyes again. I wish this girl would hurry up with my food.

Moments later, this same guy walks over with my food. When he makes it to the counter, he pauses briefly and licks his lips. So I assume this fool thought he was LL Cool J or something. I begin to think, "Can this boy give me my food so I can go?"But I can't deny how handsome he was. He had on large Jesus-piece earrings and gold rings on every finger, and he had a mouth full of Gold.

"Here you go, Beautiful. Do you need any sauce"?

"Yes, please give me some mild sauce," I replied quickly.

He bent down to a container under the counter and pulled out about 3-4 orange packets of mild sauce, which he then placed in my bag. I smiled and said thank you, and as I was about to walk out, he asked me to hold on. He then proceeded to walk from behind the counter and greet me on the other side.

"I would love to hang out with you if you are ever free; I see you work across the street," he said

"Oh really?"Why? I asked

He immediately looked confused as to why I asked him that. However, that did not deter him from continuing to connect with me.

"Well, you are beautiful, and I would love to get to know you," he said

Then he pulled out a pen, printed some receipt paper from the cash register printer, and wrote his number on it, then he handed them to me. I looked down at the receipt for this scribbled writing that read "Javari"and then his phone number.

"Thank you. I will give you a call soon," I said

He said Goodbye and rushed back behind the counter, as his coworkers were getting angry with him because the orders were starting to pile up. All of a sudden, the drive-thru had gotten very busy. As I was walking out, I looked back, and I thought he was watching me walk away.

 I giggled to myself. He looked like a street dude. I didn't know about this, but I put his number away on the side of my purse anyway. I crossed the street back to work and sat and ate my lunch before clocking back in.

As I ate, I took my phone out to save Javari's number. I was going to call him maybe in a few days to make him think I wasn't going to call. I also didn't want him to think I was thirsty and just itching to call him. My co-worker and my friend walked over and sat down with me.

"Hey girl, what's up,"she said, all goofy.

Shae and I were the manager's favorite employees. We were young, vibrant, hard-working, and dependable. The other plus was that we were both so goofy and it was lots of fun while we worked. So, as she sat and began to giggle, I just started laughing for no reason, just looking at her.

"Hey, I got this boy's number today from across the street," I said excitedly.

"Across the street where"??? She asked

I pointed across the street towards the Taco Bell and said, "The Taco Bell is over there."

"Oh, give me the details!"she said anxiously while getting close to me as if she was going to miss out on some exclusive information.

I giggled, looking at how in tune she had become. So I just got it over with, she wouldn't let me go without giving her what she wanted.

"Well, it's a boy over there named Javari. I know it sounds like a girl's name, but yes, it is indeed a boy. He is quite handsome, but he has all these Golds and stuff ... I don't know,"I said.

The look on her face was like a shell shock. Then she smiled,"Girl, I know Javari,"and kind of began to brush off the whole topic.

"Wait a minute, How do you know him"? I asked in a concerned way.

She took a deep breath in and then rolled her eyes, Sat back in the booth we were sitting at in the restaurant.

"Hmmm, where should I start?"

"Let's just go for the beginning," I said, getting a bit anxious.

"That was my old boyfriend we dated."She said,

"Oh really, well, this number is going in the trash.

She grabbed my hand at the table and said, "Girl, no, talk to him, I don't care."It wasn't like that. You can see where it goes.

I felt pretty weird and kind of confused. You know, that girl code to never

17

date someone your friend has been with or dated? However, Shae was telling me to go ahead and talk to him. I was going to take a minute to think about this instead of just making a quick decision. I folded his number back up and put it in my purse.

"Ok, if you insist," I said.

My lunch was almost over, so I opened my tacos to take a bite, I took a few bites and rushed to clock back in. This was my last night working before going on vacation. My family was going to Miami, FL, to my Uncle Jr. and Aunt Jackie's house for the weekend. All my stuff was already packed and waiting for me when I got home. So we would just be getting on the road early that morning.

At the end of my shift, I packed up and started walking toward the parking lot. I sat in the car for a minute and decided to add Javari's number to my phone address book. I wouldn't dare to call until about Sunday. Today was Thursday, so that would make it seem like I was super busy. After saving the number, I crumpled the paper and dropped it outside my car.

That morning, my family and I were on the road to Miami, and we all arrived safely. The family was just hanging out and having a good time with each other. We went out to restaurants and movies and played several board and card games once we arrived back at the house. My uncle Jr. loved jazz music and old school jams, so he played a combination of both as we interacted with one another.

On that Sunday morning, we all got up and enjoyed breakfast that my granny cooked for everyone and then we all sat and watched a movie. My uncle always had all the latest electronic gadgets, so watching movies in his living room was really like being in the actual movie theater. It was really loud as it was filled with action-packed scenes of Car racing and shooting and some fighting. Since everyone was occupied with the movie. I slipped to the room in the back where I was sleeping.

I grabbed my phone off the charger and went through my contacts. I finally came to the name I had been thinking about all day. "Javari,"I whispered to myself. I stared at the number on my screen for a minute until I finally got the courage to dial out. I hit the call button, and the phone begins to ring. I held the phone nervously, I was unsure if he would answer. I was about to hang up around the fourth ring, then a deep voice answered on the other end.

Hello"? He said "Hey, Javari"? I asked and then waited for a response.

"Hey, who's this"? He asked

"This is Ashley, You know, the Girl from Boston Market that works across the street- I explained before being cut off.

"I remember you, sexy. Hold on real quick," he replied

I was smiling from ear to ear. All I could remember was how he looked at me as I walked out of that Taco Bell that day. It was the look in his eyes, as if he loved every part of what he saw. His desire to talk to me gave me more confidence. It made me feel like something; I just didn't know what.

His background had a lot of noise and sounded as if he was around a large crowd of people. I couldn't tell if he was at work or was at some sort of BBQ gathering.

Then suddenly, it was dead silent until he began talking again.

"I've been waiting for you to call for a minute. I thought I would have to come looking for you, girl,"he said while laughing.

I giggled. "Oh really," I'm sorry I have been so busy these days."

I wasn't busy at all; I just didn't want to seem like a thirsty creep itching to call him.

"My bad, I've been working like crazy and going out of town a lot,"I said nervously.

"It's all good. Well, when are you returning from Miami? We need to link up then, sweetie."

"I will be leaving tomorrow but will be free sometime next week," I said

Before we could finalize the details about this meetup, I could hear someone yelling Javari's name in the background. Then he quickly said we would talk later, and he had to go. We both hung up the line and assumed he would get back to me. He wasn't busy because I was not calling him back until he called me.

I returned to the living room, where everyone else watched the movie, and sat down. As soon as I sat down, Javari texted me. It Read: "Next week, let's go to the movies when we both have OJT. Remember "On the Job Training"was when we could leave school earlier and head straight to work. However, Javari & my shift did not start until the evening time, around 5:30 pm or 6:00 pm. So we had part of the day to hang out once we left school around 11 am. until our shift started later. I was looking forward to hanging out with him.

I quickly texted back, saying, "o.k, that will be nice, I will let you know as soon as I make it back to Tampa." Now, all of a sudden, I was ready for this trip to be over, I wanted to hurry and get back to Tampa to see Javari. The rest of the weekend was pretty boring, too, anyway, I mean, we went to the outlet shops, had lunch, and then back to the house, but it was nothing major to brag about while in Miami.

It was now Sunday. Thank God! It was time for us to go home. All of us started packing all of our things and making sure we had all our luggage together. We packed the car and said our farewells, gave hugs and kisses, and then immediately got on the road. I was so relieved to be finally going home. It didn't take us long for us to arrive. It was about four hours later, and we were all in Tampa. We all went to our grandparent's house because that is where everyone met before we all got into the van to head to Miami.

No one went inside. We just gathered our stuff, placed it in the trunks of our cars, and were all headed home. That Sunday flew right by me. It had been an eventful weekend, and now it was back to the basics of school and work.

Javari and I had plans to hang out, and once my third period came around, I was greeted by my phone buzzing away in my pocket. I hope it was who I thought it was. I struggled for a minute to get it out of my pocket because my jeans were so tight. It was kind of sucking the life out of my legs, and that was it. I finally got the phone in my hand and glanced at the name. As I thought, It was Javari.

I answered with a huge smile on my face.

"Hello"? I answered.

"Yo wassup girl," He said

I could picture his face while he said that, and I immediately felt butterflies in my stomach. I began to giggle because when nervous, I became shy and extremely goofy.

"So, what are our plans for today"? I asked

"Swing by and pick me up, we can go to the mall, grab something to eat, and go from there, I guess. Said Javari.

"Alright, where do you want me to meet you"?

"My house, the address is 123 E. Main Street. Tampa, FL 33610

"Ok, see you in like 15 minutes, I hung up and began to walk to my car at the back of the school's parking lot. As I was walking, my best friend Myra stopped me, she wanted to ride with me to get food before work. I had to decline quickly and think of a good lie because I didn't want her to know my real plans. She was the type to ask you a million questions about everything!

When I told her, "Not today,"she looked puzzled and confused but didn't question me. Her face said it all: She was wondering what I was up to, but today, for some reason, she didn't bother to ask.

I got in the car, put my book bag and purse on the passenger side chair, and turned my radio to 98.7 FM. This was the radio station that played the latest R&B and Hip Hop hits. I put my seat belt on and then headed to Javari's house. He told me it was only 5-7 minutes away from my high school. He was right because I got there fairly quickly. I pulled up to a yellow house with a huge yard. The panels on the home were white. The side back door was white as well and had a little peek window at the top of it. The home was gated with a gray short fence.

I texted him I was outside, and about two minutes later, Javari was outside his back door, locking it and then walking down the steps. He looked very handsome, too. He had on a red shirt with some army fatigue pants and some red Nikes. I had never seen him in regular clothes. Every time I saw him, he was in his work uniform, so this was a great first impression. He smiled while walking toward me, and I gave a little smirk back.

When he got in the car, the aroma of his cologne devoured my car. He reached over and gave me a hug. We then drove to the mall, grabbed lunch and ice cream, and sat in the parking lot talking. It was really fun. We were having so much fun that it seemed as time crept upon us. It was already 5 p.m.

We both had to be at work soon, so we hopped in the car and drove to work. I pulled up to his job first, and before he got out of the car, he leaned in to kiss me. Javari's lips were so big that he left a wet spot above my lips.
I wiped it off without him looking and told him goodbye. He quickly walked into work, and then I headed to work right across the street.

In the upcoming weeks, we were together daily for almost a month. We hung out a lot. We went to the movies, to restaurants, to the park, and to shopping. We did anything you could think of.

Then of course, we were at Javari's house alone and were watching music videos on his T.V. I remember it like it was yesterday. Jim Jones ``We Fly High"by hip-hop artist Jim Jones began to play. That was my jam. I began to recite the lyrics, and Javari looked up at me, kind of surprised.

"What do you know about that girl?"He asked

I smiled and kept rapping. We both laughed, and then Javari came closer to me and began to make out with me. Javari was known to be with older women so this explained why he was so experienced with making out. The way he kissed me was different, and the way he was rubbing my leg was all different for me.

I quickly got caught in the moment because, before I knew it, Javari and I were having sex in his room.

I did come to my right mind shortly after and stopped him,

"Wait, where is your protection," I asked.

He jumped up and ran over to his dresser. He anxiously pulled out the first drawer and rambled around things in the dresser. It was clear it was nothing in that dresser, how bad he was on a scavenger hunt. I sat there patiently.

I was sure he would probably find a condom, being he was adamant about it being in his dresser. After about three minutes of no luck, he looked at me and shrugged his shoulders. He offered to leave and go to the store. I rolled my eyes. Javari didn't even have his driver's license and whose car he would drive???

Not my car! He then walked over back to the bed where I was lying down. He must have known I was waiting for some type of answer. He just began to kiss me and whispered that we would be good and that he would "Pull Out."

I was already too caught up, and it was too late to turn back now. His cologne smells so good, too. I briefly stopped him and said, "You better do what you said!"
He nodded and agreed he would follow through with his promise. So, of course, we began to have sex, and not even minutes before it ended, I had

huge regrets. I think Javari did pull out as he said he would, but I really couldn't tell. I started beating myself up that I had only known him for about 6 weeks or so, and I had already let him get the most valuable thing that belonged to me.

He stood before me, asked if I was ok, and gave me a hug and a kiss on my cheek. We both rushed to get dressed before anyone came home and knew what we were up to. After that, we went to Gyro's right by his house to get some wings and fries. Well, Javari ordered a fully loaded burger and fries.

 He always seemed to manage to ask for my food when he had his own, so he had a few wings as well. As much as this boy ate, you would think he would have picked up some weight somewhere, but he never did. He was about 6 '0 and as skinny as ever. As soon as we were done with our food, both of us got the itis.

You know the feeling of "sleepy-time"and need a nap after becoming full. We both had to be to work later, so I told Javari to take a 1-2 hour nap, then we could head to work. He took me up on my offer. We both took a shower then got in the bed in his room. About an hour and a half later, we both woke up to his mother standing over us, yelling at us.

"Javari, who is this you have in my house?"she screamed.

Javari was trying to wake up so he didn't answer right away fully. I jumped up and began to tug at Javari to get up.

"Oh, Ma, this is just my friend," he said, irritated, being sleepy, and still lying there.

"Well, baby, you have to go. I don't have anybody in my house when I'm not home,"she said while looking directly at me.

"Yes, ma'am,"I responded and got out of bed.

Javari followed my lead and got up. I walked to the living room, and he began to put on his uniform for work. I could get dressed at work later. I was just ready to get out of his house. There was no telling what his mom would do to me for being in her house when she wasn't home. Finally, Javari leaves the room and signals to go out the back door with him.

I got up quickly, with my keys ready in my hand, and opened the door and made it to my car. I opened the passenger side door for Javari, and he jumped in. I began to cruise down the road. There was an awkward silence in the car for a while, and then Javari took my hand.

"You good?" he asked me.

I didn't respond, but I nodded my head.

"Don't mind my mom, she won't even remember any of this tomorrow". He was so sure.

I just knew his mom was going to hate me for life! I was just happy to be out of there, that's all.
I told him I never wanted to go inside his mother's house when she wasn't home because I didn't want her to stop liking me. He understood and agreed to just hang out at other places if necessary.

Soon, we pulled up to Taco Bell, he leaned in to kiss me, I kissed him back with a quick peck, and I drove to work. I took a minute to sit in the car and process what happened just hours before. Javari really knew his stuff, I felt like a little toddler compared to him. He seemed as if he had a lot of practice to get the skills he had in the sex department. I had been abstinent for over two years, and I just ruined it all by having sex today. At this point it was water under the bridge.

CHAPTER 16 - SINGLE MOM OF MULTIPLE

For the upcoming weeks, Javari & I were out daily, we were glued at the hips. Meeting up after school was our normal routine for almost two months. Our school was having a fashion show, and I invited him as a guest. A lot of the students at my school already knew Javari. Especially the girls. He was very popular, and all the girls wanted to be with him. They were so annoying. The way they said, "Hey Javaarrriiii,"irked my nerves. I didn't know how popular he was until he stepped foot on our campus. Everyone was stopping him as if he were some celebrity or something.

Before we pulled up, Javari complained of having a bad headache, but he still came to support me. I grabbed my purse and gave him some Tylenol. He didn't look too good, but he was a good sport for me, and that meant a lot. I offered to take him home to get some rest and lie down, but he kept refusing. He was insisting on going to the fashion show with me.

After parking the car, I gave him a quick kiss and a hug and headed to the auditorium where the fashion show would be held. I went to the back and changed into my attire. I was really nervous. All of a sudden, I was regretting even inviting him. I no longer wanted to participate in the fashion show. I wore a white long formal gown and some nice silver heels. I could hear them call my name. The curtain was pulled back, and the bright lights glared directly into my eyes. I mustered up enough courage to walk out. I smiled but kept my eye on the wall straight ahead of me.

I could hear the school having small talk and them rating my outfit and the way I looked. From their conversations, Some liked it, and some didn't. I didn't really care, I just wanted to get off this stage. As I walked down the runway, I continued to smile, but my heart was about to fall out of my chest! I quickly turned around and walked back, waving at random people in the crowds. They began to clap for me. This boosted my confidence and made me feel a whole lot better. I finally made it to the back, and I changed into my next outfit as my other classmates ripped the runway with their outfits.

After about an hour, the fashion show was over. All of us stood on stage and bowed toward the crowd. As they clapped and cheered us on. I had to admit, although I was scared at first. I really did enjoy myself. One thing that I couldn't forget though, I caught Javari laughing when I was walking down in my second formal dress. He clearly didn't like it and then thought that it would be a good idea to laugh, I guess. I would ask him about this later.

My classmates and I are all headed back to put on our regular clothes. The talent show was over, and I still had a few hours before it was time to clock in for work. I begin to gather my belongings, including my duffel bag, shoes, and other accessories.

Once I had everything all packed up, I began to walk towards the car. While walking, I would look around, hoping to find Javari so we could go. Of course, he was nowhere to be found. I wasn't going to worry myself. I knew he was probably in some female face like always. I continued to my car. As I arrived, I put my things in the backseat. I sat there for maybe five minutes, then I crunk my car up. If Javari wanted to hang out then that meant he could find his own way home or to work.

I put the car in reverse and began to pull off. Right when I was driving away I could hear someone screaming my name.

"Ash! Hey, Ash!"The voice yelled

I looked in my rearview mirror. It was this fool Javari running after my car. I slammed on the brakes, and he caught up to the car and opened the door. I sped off as soon as he closed the door. Not even giving him time to put on his seatbelt.

"Whoah, you alright girl"? He asked.

"Am I alright? I repeated sarcastically. "Does it look like I'm alright? First, you laughed at me during the talent show and then in all these girls' faces saying God knows what!

Javari began to laugh hysterically."Man, what are you talking about," he asked.

This is one thing I hated about him: Everything was always so funny, even if something hurt my feelings.

After he got the picture that nothing was funny, he finally began to act right and apologized while trying to hug me. Then he laid his chair back while I headed to his house. Not even seconds later, he jumped up while signaling me to stop the car. I quickly pulled the car over on the side of the road, he opened the door, stuck his head outside, and began to vomit on the ground. I was shocked! I guess he was really sick, and I had an attitude with the boy.

I rubbed his back and grabbed a few napkins from my glove box that I had leftover from McDonald's the other day. I passed it to him to wipe his mouth. When he sat up, he looked over at me and said

"I think you're pregnant. Been sick like this all week."

I looked at him in utter shock, "Pregnant"?? Umm no. There is no way I am pregnant just from those couple of times."I don't know who I was trying to convince, either him or myself. When he was OK I pulled up to his house and told him to call out from work. I told him he needed plenty of fluids and to get some rest, and I would check on him after work tonight. He got out of the car and headed into the house.

I drove off and started to head to my grandparent's house. I sat over there for only a little while. I went in to say hey and bye, and that was pretty much it. Soon after, I went to work. That night, while at work, I told my friend Mayra what Javari had said earlier about me being pregnant. She was so scared for me. She kept asking me what I was going to do. The funny thing is, I couldn't answer her because I didn't know. I was only eighteen and would have two kids! My mom was going to kill me for real this time.

"Ash, well, first, you need to do a test. You don't even know if you are really pregnant and stressing for nothing," said Mayra

She was right. I didn't even confirm pregnancy and was already hoping for the worst. From that point, I just went on with my usual, not even thinking about being pregnant any longer. I finished my work at night and called Javari on my way home. He said he was feeling a little better but was still tired, so I let him get back to bed as I headed home.

When I got home, Tiyrel was still up to greet me. These terrible two of mine were a true handful! "Mommy! He would scream, "Mommy!" as soon as I entered the door.

"Hey, mommy baby,"I said as I picked him up and gave him a million kisses all over. I loved him so much. I started his bath because my mom said he had already eaten. After getting him in and out of the tub, I put both of us to bed. I was exhausted, and I had a long day ahead of me.

The next morning, Tiyrel and I got dressed. After that I dropped him off at my grandmother's. I was sure to make sure his bag was fully packed and that he had everything he needed. My Grandmother was the type to bring your baby wherever you were if he wasn't dressed or had something missing. She had proven this many times before, so I dared not to try her.

After getting him settled with my grandma, I headed off to school. I made an appointment to meet with my guidance counselor once more. Graduation was approaching soon, and I needed to know where I stood. My grandma was rooting for me, and she would always tell me to get my education! She had to drop out of high school to start working to help her parents bring income into the home.

That is why she was so adamant about me finishing. She wanted me to have a better future and a better life than she did. She was forced to do hard labor cleaning for pennies because she didn't finish school, which pushed me even more. I wanted to make my grandmother proud.

As I pulled into the school, I went straight to Mrs. Poole's office. I signed in and then had a seat, waiting for her to call my name. I could hear her walking from her office, her heels left behind a lingering click-clack in the hallway.

"Ashley Montgomery,"she called.

I jumped up and ran over to her. I was smiling ear to ear. She began to roll her eyes. Ms. Montgomery, I hope you are ready to hear what I have to say today, she stated very sternly, not a bit impressed by my overjoyed energy.

"Mrs. Poole, I came all the way up here to see you, and this is what I get in return?"I asked.

She couldn't help but give me a little smirk anyway. I would take that as long as I made one person smile, that is what gave me life!

As we walked to her office, Mrs. Smith's office was on the left side, and she was sitting in there looking over some paperwork. Her glasses were half down her face as she read over her documents.

"Mrs. Smith, Mrs Smith" I chanted, as she looked over her glasses.

I knew it had to be Ms. Montgomery! You are the loudest student here at King High,"she laughed.

"I will take that as a compliment, Mrs. Smith,"I said while winking my eyes at her.

Finally, we made it to Mrs. Poole's office. I sat down, and Mrs. Poole sat behind her desk and grabbed a folder with my name on it. She opened it and then began to go over my grades and all of my credits. She explained that I had been doing a great job in my current classes.

Then she paused and gave this serious look before asking this question.

"Do you want me to give the bad news first or the good news first, Ash?" she asked.

I took a deep breath in/ out and said, "Give me the bad."

She then dropped the bomb on me, having to retake Biology for the third time. I hated that class. For one, I wasn't dissecting a frog, no pig, NO NOTHING! That was disgusting. I had no interest in that class and didn't understand why my time was being wasted there. The next bad news was that I still needed an English 4 credit as well. Those were two core classes and I would not have them completed in time by graduation.

My entire attitude and mood changed immediately. I felt like a failure. I knew I had played in school my ninth and tenth-grade years, but I straightened up and was in class every day getting my work done. I was so mad at myself! Mrs. Poole saw the look of despair in my eyes and tried to encourage me.

"Ash, I know you won't walk with the class of 2007, however, you will still graduate this summer if you go ahead and complete these two classes in night school." Then she continued to say that my GPA was 2.5, so I was on track with everything else. My grandmother was looking forward to going to my graduation. She had already told all her friends about me walking on the stage. I hated that I was disappointing her and also my mother. My mom always cared what people thought about her, especially her children so that she would be furious with this news.

I then stood up, I had enough. I told Mrs.Poole to have a nice day, and I walked towards the exit doors of the guidance office. For the rest of the day, I was in a slump. I didn't talk much to anyone. I went to the restroom before heading to class. I put my back against the door after locking it and began to cry softly. Everyone was going to laugh and make fun of me, and I was going to miss the biggest day of my life!

I got myself together and finished the day at school. I suffered from a bad migraine. I couldn't eat my lunch. I also found myself being so aggravated with everything and everybody. I had a nasty attitude just out of nowhere. That day, I skipped seeing Javari. I don't remember what excuse I made up not to see him, but I went straight to work from school. I knew they could use an extra worker around this time.

As soon as I pulled in, Shae and my other coworker, Brittany, came outside to greet me. They even knew something was off with me. I was really short, not my normal funny, bubbly self. I just told them I didn't feel good. Shae gave me a side eye and asked me in my ear, "Did you do the pregnancy test, Ash?"

I had totally forgotten about possibly being pregnant. I had too much going on. I proceeded to tell her no in hopes she would just leave it alone. However, she didn't leave it alone. She said I was looking different these days, and she thought it would be best if I did it. I wanted her to leave me alone, so I told her I would go on my lunch break and get the test at CVS, which was directly across the street from us.

Hours had passed, and it was already my lunch break. I had no money, and we weren't scheduled to get paid until that Friday. Today was Monday. How was I going to buy the pregnancy test? I had a not-so-good idea, but I did it anyway. I looked around the store to make sure the coast was clear, and I opened the cash register and slipped a $20 bill out. I forced it into my pocket quickly. Then I went and clocked out for lunch. I let Shae know where I was going, and I would be right back. I grabbed my cell phone. I was calling Mayra to let her know I was about to buy the test.

She answered, and she stayed on the phone the entire time I was in the store. She was my best friend, she told me she wouldn't hang up even if she was at work. I ran across the street, looking both ways not to get hit by a car. I made it inside. I went to the aisle that held the pregnancy tests. There were so many different options.I went for the cheapest price, which was the CVS brand pregnancy test. I took it to the front, trying to keep what I had discreet as I walked to the register.

"Hello, did you find everything ok"? asked the clerk

I was so paranoid I couldn't speak, but I nodded. She rang my item up and gave me my change. I grabbed my bag and ran out of the store back to my job. I went straight to the bathroom. She followed behind me when she saw me. She saw I had someone on the phone.

"Who's on the phone?"She asked as she closed the door behind her.

"It's Mayra, she wants to know the results too," I said.

I opened the box and read the instructions to Shae. She stood there as I took the stick out of the box. I pulled my pants down and started to pee on the stick. I quickly handed it to her. She placed the top on it and placed it on the sink. The box advised us to wait about five minutes for the results. This was the longest five minutes of my life.

I didn't want to look at the stick; I was entirely too scared. Mayra was still on the phone, she was getting antsy herself.

"Ash, what does it say"?

I had my back against the wall, waiting for Shae to look and give the news. I began to daydream that I was walking out of the bathroom with the results being, "I was not pregnant"! I couldn't be a mother of two when I was only eighteen. What was I going to do with another baby? Shae stood there with the stick in her hand. She looked down, and then she looked up at me. Her face was neutral, so I couldn't tell what it said. She then asked if I was ready.

I just stared at her, if that wasn't the dumbest question. I don't think I would ever be ready. She then turned the stick facing me and screeched, "You are pregnant!"She quickly covered her mouth in fear that someone may have heard her. I just slid down the wall in disbelief! I was in an entire shock. I felt fine all this time. How could this happen AGAIN??? I had enough bad news for today. First, I'm told I'm not graduating, and then now I'm pregnant again.

Out of nowhere, we both hear a loud knock from the other side of the door. "Boom, Boom! Was the sound from the door? It was followed by a deep baritone voice "What are you girls doing in there"? My drive-thru is backed up!!!! We recognized the voice very quickly. It was our store manager Rich. I got up, Shae hid the test in the trash, and I finally opened up the door.

The look on Rich's face was like, "GET TO WORK NOW!"We didn't say a word; we just ran to the drive-thru area and began to get to work as quickly as possible. That entire night, I was just a mess. I was messing up on the customers' orders, missing items, and becoming very clumsy. Today was a very eventful day, and I wanted it all to be a joke or a prank!

As I closed the store, I called Javari. He didn't work tonight, so I told him I would stop by to see him. I ran to the bathroom before clocking out to grab the box with the pregnancy test in it. I placed it in my bookbag. I walked to the office, clocked out, and drove to Javari's house. My hands began to sweat as I was holding the steering wheel.

I didn't know how I was going to tell him this. I was so scared of how he would respond. Would he support me and be there for me and our baby? My head was filled with so many different thoughts and emotions.

Finally, I pulled up, I texted him I was outside and he came out and sat in the car. He jumped in all giddy and had this huge smile on his face. He leaned in to kiss me, and I just sat there looking scared. He backed up and wondered what was wrong.

"Yo, you alright?" he asked.

"Not really; I have something to tell you," I said in fear.

He hugged me and whispered in my ear to tell him. I took a deep breath in. Then I looked at his face. I grabbed my bookbag from the backseat, took out the box, and handed it to him. He held the box for a while without saying anything. He then looked at me briefly, still silent, and then back at the box. He opened it and then looked at the stick. He was staring at the two dark pink lines on the screen.

He nodded and said, "It's gonna be OK, I got you."

I was so surprised, his reaction was not what I expected. I thought he was going to be spazzing out. He gave me another hug. He assured me that everything would be ok and not to worry. He took a huge weight off of my shoulders. I had peace, and I felt much better. He was going to be there for me. This was already going better than when I discovered I was pregnant with Tiyrel.

I gave him a kiss and then told him I should get home, but we would talk when I got home. Before he got out of the car, I told him not to tell anybody until we figured out what we were going to say together. He agreed with me. He got out of the car and headed into the house.

On the ride home, I blasted my R&B jams. I was having another baby! My grandma, mom, and granddad were going to hit the roof! It had been over three years, so hopefully, they would think of it that way. As I pulled up in my yard, Javari was already calling me. He had the amount of time it took for me to be home down-packed, I thought to myself. I turned off my car and sat there as I answered the phone.

"Hello"? I answered

"Hey," Javari said

"I just got home, You were right on time!"

"Oh yeah, that's cool. Well, I need to tell you something. He said

"Ok, what's up?

"My mama said I'm not doing anything for that baby until I get a DNA test!"

My heart sank immediately! I could hardly breathe, and my heart began to beat so fast.

"What do you mean, Javari," I asked
He didn't give me an answer and hung up the phone right in my face!

I began to beat my hands on the steering wheel! Not again! Not again! Not again! I screamed over and over! What made Javari switch up on me this quickly!? I sobbed in the car for a while, and then I saw someone come to the door. It was Ernesto.

I think he saw my headlights on but didn't see me walk in the house. I began to get out of the car, grabbing my bookbag. I wiped my eyes really quickly so he wouldn't see me crying.

As I walked to the porch, Ernesto was smiling.

"What's up Girl, how was work"?

When I got closer, he knew something was wrong immediately and stopped me.

"Hey, what's wrong"? He asked.

I sat on the bench on the porch and he followed me and sat there as well. I told him I was pregnant again from Javari, and I told him what he said and that he wasn't going to be there. He grabbed me and hugged me. I sat there and continued to cry. Ernesto, in the moment, gave me the words I needed to hear.

"Ash, it's okay. You got me to help you. Don't worry about him. We will get through this!"Now wipe your eyes, or else your mom is going to find out, and you already know how that is going to be.

I said o.k, and we both went into the house. I went straight to the shower. I needed to get my thoughts together. I was going to be a mother AGAIN for the second time.

I appreciated Ernesto at that moment for listening to me and being understanding. He also kept a secret of mine until I was willing to share. He also had Tiyrel all settled in and tucked into bed for me. Ernesto was an amazing grandfather with him. Tiyrel loved him so much. There was nothing he wouldn't do for my baby. That did mean a lot because, as you already know, my biological dad was never around.

CHAPTER 17: MOVING OUT

The news of my second pregnancy spread like wildfire, and soon everyone knew. This time, though I was eighteen and older, the reactions were mixed. My uncle Jr, a perpetual pessimist, always had a way of dampening my spirits. He seemed to take joy in casting doubt on my future, betting against my success as if there were a prize for betting against me. His negativity weighed heavily on me, chipping away at my confidence and leaving me questioning my own abilities.

My mom's disappointment was palpable, a constant reminder of my desire to make her proud. Her happiness meant everything to me, and I longed to see her smile. Yet, it seemed like no matter what I did, she remained upset with me. Even on days when I hadn't crossed her, her frustration found its way to me. Living under her roof, I yearned for independence, craving the chance to forge my own path.

The decision to move out weighed heavily on me, but I knew it was necessary. With my brother gone and my mom preoccupied with her husband and church activities, I felt increasingly isolated. Despite his role as a doting grandparent to Tiyrel, I harbored concerns about my mom's husband. His behavior, coupled with my mom's transformation in his presence, left me feeling like a stranger in my own home.

For one, my brother was already gone and moved out, so I felt all alone. The next reason was to get away from my mom and her husband. Although he was the best grandparent my son Tiyrel had, things about him worried me. My mom, on the other hand, just became a different person when she got with her husband. It became more and more about him and her church functions than us (her children).

I remember like it was yesterday.......

My mother came home from work at her typical time, and she would do her normal. Get undressed, shower, put on a slip, and then grab a bite to eat. Ernesto had been in the kitchen earlier and left a huge mess on the counter. When my mom came into the kitchen, she was upset about the kitchen.

The area was in a mess from what he left behind. He literally ate and left his plate, silverware, and snack wrapper papers just all over the counter.

35

She began to yell, asking why her kitchen looked like this. I peeked in and said, "Your husband left that mess, Ma."

She then looked at me as if what I said was a crime. The tension simmered beneath the surface, evident in every interaction with my mom. Her reaction to my pregnancy seemed to trigger a visceral response, casting a shadow over our relationship. When she demanded I clean up Ernesto's mess, I stood there dumbfounded, incredulous at the unfairness of it all. But silence was no longer an option; I had to speak up.

"Ma, your husband made that mess, and I'm not cleaning it up!"

At that moment, I refused to play along with the facade of infallibility surrounding her husband. But my defiance only fueled her fury.

"I don't care who did it, Come and clean this mess up"!

I retreated to the living room, daring to challenge her authority.

"No, I'm not cleaning up a grown man's mess, You clean it up, you are his wife aren't you?"

My words sparked an intense anger in her, like lighting a match to gasoline. She swiftly crossed the kitchen and struck me on the side of my head. I was shocked and defenseless, wondering why she had turned to violence. Amidst the chaos, I stayed strong, shielding myself with my arms until her anger faded.

Her sudden call to the authorities startled me into action, and I hurried to my room as her words echoed through the house.

"Yes, can you please send an officer to 1234 S. 85th Street? My daughter is fighting me."

The accusation weighed heavily on me, sending shockwaves through my core. Rushing back to confront her, I sought clarity amidst the chaos.

"Mom, why are you telling the police I'm fighting you? I never touched you"!

But my protests were ignored as she silenced me with a stern demand. Feeling defeated, I retreated to my room, weighed down by her betrayal. Tiyrel sensed my distress and approached with innocent curiosity, his concern clear in his gaze.

"What's wrong, Mommy?" His words cut through the tension, offering a brief respite from the turmoil.

"Nothing, baby," I reassured him, holding him close in a tight embrace, shielding him from the storm brewing outside our door.

As time passed, the tension in the air grew thicker. When law enforcement arrived, the drama escalated further, my mother spinning lies to justify her actions.

Summoned to tell my side, I braced myself for what awaited outside the door. Stepping into the harsh light of reality, I was met by a white officer, his stern gaze cutting through the tension.

Called out to explain, I prepared myself for what was waiting beyond the door. Stepping into the harsh reality outside, a white officer met me with a serious look.

"Are you Ashley Montgomery?" His voice cut through the tension, hinting at what was coming next.

"Yes," I managed, my voice showing my growing unease.

In a quick move, he informed me I was under arrest and put handcuffs on me, his actions shocking me.

"Arrested?!" The words came out in a desperate plea for clarity, but there was no relief—only the cold steel of the handcuffs on my skin.

As he read me my rights, I stood still, feeling the gravity of the moment weigh heavily on me. Led outside, I was overcome with disbelief and hurt. How could my own mother betray me like this?

Seated in the back of the police car, tears streamed down my face, silently expressing the injustice I felt. When the officer handed a paper to my mother, I pulled away attempting to hide, desperate to protect my son from the painful truth unfolding before us.

With a serious handoff, the officer gave the paper to my mom as we headed to the police station. Every moment felt like forever, my heart pounding. When we entered the garage, the gate closed behind us, sealing our fate. Surrounded by police cars, we walked toward the intimidating blue doors.

The officer unlocked the door with his badge, and we entered a large room with rows of blue chairs. To the right, officers stood behind windows with glowing computer screens. Above them hung a bright blue sign that said: BOOKING.

After passing through a metal detector and being patted down by a female officer, my handcuffs were finally taken off. Called to the booking window, I faced a remarkably pretty woman. Her smile didn't match the seriousness of where we were.

"Hey there, what's a young lady like you doing in a place like this?" she asked, her warm smile contrasting with the cold surroundings.

I didn't feel pretty or calm then; I was angry and frustrated. But I answered her. Her kindness was surprising and strangely reassuring, easing some of my fear and anxiety.

"It's a long story," I sighed, my voice betraying both apprehension and frustration.

She went on to ask for my personal details—full name, date of birth, address, phone number, even where I worked. Each question felt like an invasion of privacy, making me even more uneasy. Why did she need all this information?

Reluctantly, I provided what she asked for and was then directed to the next checkpoint.

Approaching the next window marked "FINGERPRINTING," I placed my palms flat on the scanning surface. The officer, wearing gloves, carefully rolled each of my fingers, capturing my prints with a small camera.

After that, I was led to a section where I had to change clothes, probably into inmate uniform. The outfit looked like scrubs: orange pants and tops with "Property of ORJ" printed on the back. They also gave me thick white socks and brown slippers.

My belongings were packed and labeled with my name before being handed to another staff member. They then placed it on a shelf among other inmates' belongings.

Following that, I was directed to meet with a nurse to discuss my medical history and any health concerns I might have had. Subsequently, I was ushered to the back along with others who had been arrested. As we entered a large room with individual cells, all eyes turned towards us. The guard provided us with a set of rules, distributed towels and sheets, and guided us to our designated cells.

After settling into my cell, I hurried downstairs to use the phone. I was desperate to ascertain how long I would be confined. I reached out to my grandma, knowing she would assist in getting me out. When she accepted the call, relief flooded over me. Thank heavens!

"Hey, Grandma!" I exclaimed with excitement.

"Ash?" she responded.

"Yes, Grandma, it's me."

"Now, how in the world did you end up in jail?" she inquired.

"Your daughter, Grandma, got me in here. I just want to come home. Can you check and see if someone can get me out?" I pleaded.

Before I could receive her response, a guard with a booming voice called out my last name, followed by a number.

"Montgomery 6-3-6-9?" they repeated.

I had to abruptly end my conversation with my grandma and stride towards the guard calling my name. The female guard had a stern expression on her face. She was hefty and looked strong, instilling a sense of fear in me. It appeared I was already in trouble.

"Are you Montgomery?" she asked firmly.

"Yes, ma'am, that's me," I replied, bracing myself for what was to come.

The entire pod fell into a heavy silence, every eye fixated on me as if I were the center of some gripping drama. My heart pounded against my chest, threatening to break free as panic surged through me. The guard's instruction to ascend the stairs to my cell echoed in my ears, her presence behind me feeling like a threatening, shadow. When I finally reached my cell, I stood frozen at the door, meeting her gaze with fear.

Her pointed finger directed my attention to the untidy bed, her words cutting through the tense air, "You didn't make your bed; you just ran to the phone."

The realization hit me like a punch in the gut—I hadn't even known I was supposed to make the bed,I was left to fumble with the blankets and sheets without any guidance.

As I obediently began to straighten the linens, the guard sealed the door behind me with a resounding click, the room enveloped in a somber darkness. With each tug of the sheets, tears streamed down my cheeks, my sobs echoing off the sterile walls. All I longed for in that moment was to escape, to return to the safety of home. It was then, amidst my despair, that I found myself wishing I had mustered the courage to clean up Ernesto's mess after all.

The hours felt never-ending in that cell at night. I was hungry, with hunger gnawing at my insides, and my throat was dry from thirst. When daylight finally filtered through the narrow window, it felt like an eternity had passed. Then, like a beacon of hope, a new guard arrived, the metallic clang of keys signaling my impending release. With each step towards freedom, anticipation surged through me like a current, electrifying every nerve.

As I stepped back into the familiar processing area, relief washed over me like a tidal wave. The burden of being locked away began to ease, replaced by the hope of freedom. They handed me my bag of clothes—a tangible symbol of reclaiming my life—and I eagerly dressed, ready to reenter the outside world.

Amidst the whirlwind of emotions, an unexpected sight greeted me—my mother. Her presence was a surprise, one I hadn't anticipated. Yet, in the midst of this emotional storm, words failed me. Uncertainty hung over me like a shadow, leaving me silent as I settled into the passenger seat of my grandmother's van.

The journey home passed in silence, each mile weighed down by unspoken words and unanswered questions. In that quiet moment, a sense of acceptance settled over me.

Who was I to challenge the hand that fate had dealt me? It was a burden I had grown accustomed to carrying, the heavy weight of life's uncertainties pressing down upon me.

I didn't realize it then, but the break from challenges wouldn't last long. When I entered our home office again, I was about to face the next part of my tough journey, ready to test how strong I really was.

The quiet of the house was broken by the sound of Ernesto's footsteps getting louder as he approached the room where I was. Even though I hadn't turned around yet, I could feel him staring at me. So, I finally asked, "Hey Ernesto, what's up?" He just laughed and said nothing much.

When I turned around, I saw him holding out a crumpled piece of paper. It seemed strange, but I took it anyway

After grabbing the crumpled paper, Ernesto walked away. I carefully unfolded it and found something alarming inside: a white powdered substance and a short letter. I brushed some of the powder aside to read the message, which said, "I can give you ANYTHING you need"!

Confusion and anger surged through me. Why was Ernesto giving me a white powdery substance that was clearly some type of drug, and what did he mean by "anything"? I clenched the paper tightly, feeling lost in a whirlwind of emotions.

Suddenly, I heard the garage door opening. My mother was home!

She had arrived just in the nick of time. As I listened, the sound of Tiyrel's laughter echoed through the house, followed by the unmistakable sound of him bounding towards the garage door. It was clear he had reunited with Ernesto, and their playful banter filled the air. Despite my own turmoil, seeing Tiyrel's happiness brought a smile to my face. His joy was everything to me.

At that moment, I couldn't help but think about the absence of my own father. Tiyrel was missing out on the presence of a grandfather(My Bio father) who could have played a significant role in his life.

Shortly after, I heard my mother's footsteps as she entered the house and greeted Tiyrel warmly.

"Okay, babe, I'll catch you later," she murmured as she closed the door to the garage. I made my way to the kitchen to join her, finding her cradling Tiyrel in her arms, showering him with affectionate hugs and kisses.

"Hey, ma," I greeted her, but the troubled expression on my face didn't go unnoticed.

"How are you doing, Ash?" she inquired, her attention shifting to me as she set Tiyrel down.

Instead of answering her question, I cut straight to the chase. "Where's Ernesto?" I asked urgently.

"He just left," she replied, her tone tinged with curiosity at my intensity.

"Good," I said briskly, as I reached into my pocket and placed the crumpled paper Ernesto had given me in the center of my mom's outstretched hand.

Confusion flickered across her face as she unfolded the paper, revealing its mysterious contents. The powdered substance inside shifted slightly, causing a small cloud to puff up into the air.

"What the heck?" she exclaimed, her brows furrowed in confusion as she scrutinized the note.

As she finished reading, I explained that her husband had handed it to me, leaving me bewildered as to why. I awaited her response, watching as her expression shifted from puzzlement to anger in an instant. Without hesitation, she snatched up the house phone and dialed Ernesto's number. From across the room, I could hear his voice on the other end, a casual "Hello" greeting.

"Ernesto, what the heck is this stuff you gave Ashley?" she demanded, her tone sharp with indignation.

Ernesto began to explain, and I couldn't help but be curious about his response. With my arms crossed, I waited anxiously as Tiyrel busied himself in the living room, completely unaware of the tension brewing. Moments later, my mom's voice floated from the phone, a resigned tone indicating the end of the conversation.

"Okay, don't do that again! Bye," she stated firmly before hanging up. I looked at her expectantly, waiting for her to relay Ernesto's explanation. As she bent

down to remove her shoes, she glanced up at me and delivered the news.

"Ernesto said he gave you that to see if you were on drugs," she explained, her words hitting me like a ton of bricks.

"What?" I exclaimed, disbelief coloring my voice. "I don't do drugs, Ma! What are you talking about?"

Well, that's what he said, Ash," she replied dismissively, already turning to walk towards her room.

I seethed with frustration. That was it? That was all she had to say? This man had handed me what appeared to be cocaine, and his excuse was a pathetic attempt to see if I was using drugs? Seriously? A simple drug test could have sufficed, couldn't it? None of it made any sense. I hadn't been in trouble recently, and I had never touched drugs in my life. Why was my mom allowing this to happen?

This was exactly the kind of thing that happened to me without explanation, leaving me to accept it silently, lest I be labeled as the angry black girl. It was infuriating. At that moment, I yearned to call my dad and pour out my frustrations to him. I needed him. Yet, even he seemed to find me unworthy of his presence in my life.

I slipped on my shoes and then Tiyrel's, grabbed my keys, and headed out for a drive. I needed some space, some fresh air. That day passed, and the incident was swept under the rug. Over the following months, life went on as usual - work, school, repeat.

I missed my graduation with the class of 2007 from King High School.. I couldn't walk across that stage because I hadn't earned all my credits in time. The thought of facing my classmates, of admitting my failure, was too much to bear. Instead, I watched the ceremony from afar, my name flashing on the screen in the Sundome, a hollow reminder of what could have been. It broke me to see my friends revel in their achievements while I remained on the sidelines. It was a stark lesson in the importance of taking academics seriously.

My family was disappointed that I didn't attend the graduation. Yet, their support remained unwavering. My grandmother, in particular, was my rock, sharing stories of her own sacrifices to inspire me. She emphasized the value of education, urging me to persevere. My mother echoed her sentiments, urging me to stay focused on my goals. Their belief in me fueled my determination to make them proud.

This time, their words resonated with me like never before, igniting a fire within me. Two months later, I achieved what once seemed impossible- I earned my high school diploma. I'll never forget the day Mrs. Poole, my guidance counselor,beckoned me to the school to collect it. I practically sprinted there, bounding up the stairs to the guidance office. Mrs. Poole and Mrs. Smith awaited me in the lobby, holding my diploma in a sleek blue folder. I snatched it from their hands, shouting triumphantly, "I DID IT!! I DID IT!!"

Their beaming smiles mirrored my own, as they applauded and embraced me. "Congratulations, Ash," they cheered. It was a moment of pure joy, one of the best in my life. Despite all the obstacles, I graduated from high school on June 25, 2007. A teenage mother to a 4-year-old and pregnant with my second child, I defied the odds and achieved my goal.

My family was overjoyed when they heard the news. As for my Uncle Jr., who had doubted me and made a $500 bet against my success, well, he ended up looking like a fool. But none of that mattered to me. I had proven to myself that I could do it, against all odds.

With my diploma in hand, I landed a better-paying job at a furniture store called "HomeNow." It specialized in rental furniture, similar to Rent-a-Center or Buddy's and Aaron's. I took on the role of front desk clerk, saving every penny for what would soon be my own place. It was time for me to spread my wings and build a life for myself and my boys.

I scoured listings for affordable apartments, determined to find a place to call our own despite earning just $9.00 an hour. Tony, Tiyrel's dad, hadn't provided any child support during my time with Javari, but he stepped up, ensuring we had what we needed for both boys. I admired his commitment and thought it made sense for him to move in with us.

After much searching, I stumbled upon Park Terrace Apartments, located off 40th Street and Hillsborough Ave. The rent for a two-bedroom, two-bathroom apartment was $604.00 in 2007. To my delight, I was approved! Yet, little did I know, adulthood came with a whole new set of challenges.

Chapter 18: On My Own

I prolonged moving out until I gave birth to my now second son, Tiyler. My grandmother and my mom were the only two in the room with me. He was born at University Community Hospital. I nicknamed him "TJ." He was born on September 7, 2007. Javari and I did not talk during my entire pregnancy.

The last I had heard of him was the night he told me he wasn't going to do anything for our son until he got a DNA test. I went to all of my appointments alone and gave birth to our son without him. That made me feel empty inside. I had this happen to me once before, and I didn't learn my lesson!

Upon being released from the hospital, Tiyrel, TJ, and I stayed with my grandparents. My grandmother would help me care for the baby for the next couple of weeks. She didn't play either. She was a real old-school granny. She made me cover my head and my feet and warned me not to be outside! She put the fear in me of having a major SETBACK after just giving birth to a baby.

Once settled in for a few days, I called Javari to let him know I had the baby. He didn't live too far from my grandmother's house, so he made his way over fairly quickly. When he arrived, he looked very handsome as usual. He was dressed to the nines and, of course, had his gold teeth and jewelry on. He stepped into my grandmother's house and had a seat. My granny went to get TJ from the back and then handed him to Javari.

I noticed at that moment Javari began to smile from ear to ear. He began to talk to him.

"What's up, little man"? He said

He was rubbing TJ's head and staring at him. He then got his phone out and began to snap a few pictures. I knew he was doing this to send to his mother. However, I was not worried. TJ came out looking EXACTLY like Javari—I mean, an exact replica! My granny couldn't help but notice how he looked just like his dad.

"Whew, young man, that is definitely your baby, it's like you spit him out"! She said laughing

He looked up at her and said, "Yes, mam, he does look like me,"and then went back to talking to TJ. I'm not going to lie; I felt much better that he actually felt differently after seeing TJ. He then asked if it would be okay if we both went over to his mother's home so she could see the baby.

I looked up at my grandma for permission. She looked like she was saying "Oh lord" in her head, but she actually said it was OK to make sure me and the baby were bundled up and to go straight to the house and back. I agreed, and we got dressed and headed over to his mom's.

When we pulled up in Javari's yard, his mom was already waiting for us on the porch on the carport.

"Where is my baby, Where is my baby?"she screamed excitedly.

Javari opened the door and said he was in the backseat. She ran over before he could open the back door and went to grab the car seat. She looked up to the front seat, where I was sitting.

"Hey Ash, how are you doing?"

I said Hello and smiled, but I couldn't help but remember her not being around or involved when I was pregnant. In fact, she was the reason her son said he wasn't going to be there until he got a DNA Test!

For now, we were just going to focus on the now, but I really wanted to say something. However, I chose just to keep my mouth shut. We all entered the house, and his mother and father were in the living room. They were mesmerized by TJ and just kept saying how much he looked just like Javari. Tj had his face, skin color, both of our slanted eyes and huge lips! I mean every time I looked at my son, I saw his dad. I had no parts in the way he looked.

We all were in the house, and Javari's mom was just having a ball with the baby. She was kissing him, hugging him, and everything. His dad would chime in every now and then, but he didn't want to hold him. He said he was way too little right now. This was so funny to me because it seemed like all the men said that with newborns.

We sat for a while longer, and then Javari took me and the baby home, but before we drove off, his mom stood in the door and said

"Oooh, Ash, you won't need a DNA test because, honey, everyone can SEE that's his baby."

I just nodded my head while saying, "yes, ma'am"......

Javari took us both back to my granny's, and he hugged and kissed me outside. He never apologized for what he said to me, how he made me feel, and what he had done to me by leaving me all alone to go through a pregnancy alone. He just acted as if it all never happened.

I can't lie—I did miss him, but I couldn't help but remember the night he abandoned me all because of a comment his mother made. He carried TJ's car seat to the door, and we went inside. My granny was already in the den, waiting for us to return. I could tell she was ready for me to give her the rundown on what happened when we were gone. I was ready, too.

She thanked Javari for bringing us back safe and sound, and we told him goodbye.

Shortly after, I felt my granny in on how Javari's mom said they no longer wanted a DNA test and was saying how much the baby looked like him. My granny rolled her eyes swiftly and gave a deep breath in.

"They are still getting a DNA test, don't you ever let no man's mama have the audacity to say her son is not your child's father"NEVER!

She was adamant about that. I agreed with her, though. His mom wasn't there, so how could she just judge me like that just because I already had a son? It really didn't matter at this point, because this was evident what the truth was.

Over the next couple of months, Javari and I communicated more, and he really stepped up to the plate to help me with TJ. We eventually decided to get back together. I had already been approved for an apartment; I was just waiting to get a move-in date. I asked Javari to move in with me and the boys, and of course, he took me up on my offer.

We had finally moved out of my mom's home. I bought all of my furniture from a local consignment shop. It was so funny, none of the pieces matched at all. I had one floral sofa, a green couch, and an orange accent chair. I finished the living room setting by adding a three piece table set. It consisted of a crystal glass coffee table and two end tables.

My dining room had an oak table and white and oak-colored chairs. It was a four-piece set. I bought that for $60 from a man selling furniture on the side of the road one day. He delivered it for free, too! Then, my grandmother bought my entire bedroom set from Funland Flea Market for $200.00! The set was a queen-size bed, two end tables, a mirror, and a dresser. It was Black with a Gold marble hand-painted design on it.

Lastly, I rented a red metal-frame bunk bed from a rental furniture store called Buddys. They offered free delivery and set-up as well. This is when I met one of my now best male friends, Thomas. He was a very nice gentleman. He was a tall dark chocolate husky man. He was so mannerable and respectful. We immediately hit it off, and he has been my everlasting right-hand man since that day.

My apartment was now fully furnished. I remember Javari putting money towards the move-in cost. The last thing we did was get a few groceries from a store named "Save a lot"because we were now low on cash. This was a great place to shop to get a lot for your money.

We were both on cloud-nine. We had our own place and were now real adults with real bills! I was just excited to have my own place and have the freedom to do what I wanted. I woke up when I wanted to on the weekends, I cleaned up when I wanted to, and I had NO CURFEW!!

It was a dream to have my man, my boys, and our little family. We were so young and had no idea what we were getting ourselves into. Happiness and butterflies faded away pretty quickly. Javari and I had only been in our apartment for about six weeks. I was working a new Job at a bank called "Citibank"making around $12.50 hourly. Javari was working for a construction company, and he made around $14.00/hour. For us to be only eighteen years old we were doing well.

I would watch the boys during the day until he got home at 3:15 PM and then I would leave because my shift at work was from 4:30 PM to 1:00 AM in the morning. When I used to come home at 1:00 AM I would walk into the house being in a mess a majority of the time. Javari was a big kid, so he would leave everything out, and he did not clean up after the boys. So I often had to come home to tidy up, and I would be so tired.

I would let him know, but it was no use because it would always be short-lived, so I made sure just always to get it done. From all the hours I had worked throughout the week. I would sleep in and rest up on the weekends. I was always a homebody. I didn't have many friends and I didn't go to clubs or parties etc. I was a mother, so my night consisted of changing diapers, cooking, cleaning & watching Barney & Friends, The Big Comfy Couch, and Sesame Street.

Javari, on the other hand, was always hanging out. He had friends, and he was very close to his older sister and brothers. So they would take him out, and he would be gone a lot. On the nights he wasn't going out, he would be playing the game or watching TV in the living room. I always went to bed early, so I was out around 9:30 PM every night.

This particular night, I fell asleep early but was awakened by Jamie's voice on the phone. My door was cracked and he was in the living room on the phone. I couldn't determine who was on the other end of the phone, but what I heard that night broke me.

"Oh, she always goes to bed early and sleeps hard, so she never hears anything,"he said.

Then, whatever the other person said, He responded quickly, saying: "Okay, I will be over in a little."Then they both hung up.

I quickly hurried to fake sleeping, but while peeking at our bedroom door, I saw Javari walk to our bedroom to peek in at me, and then he closed the door completely. Why was he coming to look at me? And where in the heck was he going? Right after that, I heard the front door shut. I then jumped up to look at the phone to see what time it was. My phone showed it was 11:45 PM, almost midnight!

I then ran over to my window and peeked out to see if I could see where he was going. To my surprise, he was walking, he wasn't getting in his car. And as I looked at him, he was looking up at our window. He was up to no good. As he continued to walk further on the sidewalk, I followed him by looking through our window in the living room and then the last window from the boys' rooms. Once I reached that window I could no longer see him in sight. I should have just run after him outside. But for some reason, I was scared.

I began to cry, and my heart began to race so fast. I went back to my room and grabbed my phone. The first person I thought to call was Javari's sister. She was older than us, and she always gave sound advice. Also, since they were so close, she had no problem getting Javari together if he was wrong. I dialed her and explained what was going on. She told me to come pick her up. I'm glad the boys stayed at my mom's that night, so I left to get her.

When I picked her up at that point, I was just crying hysterically. I knew Javari was cheating on me, and the most disrespectful part was he was cheating with a woman IN OUR APARTMENT COMPLEX! His sister just grabbed me and hugged me until I got myself together. Then she told me to go back to the house. We both pulled back up to the house and went inside and he still wasn't back. We waited around awhile and he never showed. It was now nearly 1:00 AM, so she had to go home. I drove her home and said goodnight.

It took me about 15-20 minutes. I came into the house and Javari was on the couch sleeping. I tiptoed to my room and got in the bed. I don't know if he came into the room to see if I was there or not while I was gone. I got under my covers and just couldn't sleep. I was in a rage! I wanted answers! However, I didn't want to make a big deal out of it. My entire childhood everyone made me the problem, so this time, I wasn't going to be the problem. I decided just to sit there and take it. I mean, this is what I see every woman in my family do. They stuck it out no matter what.

The next morning, I acted as if nothing had ever happened. I didn't mutter a word. It was Sunday, so I started to prepare for the next week. Preparing for the week consisted of me getting all the things out the boys needed, their clothes, and dinner for every night Javari would be watching them. We both continued to work and pay the bills.

However, soon Javari would start missing a lot of days of work for whatever reason. He would say he didn't feel like going to work or he was tired. He also would wake up late and his boss would be looking for him. He wanted to be home with me during the day, I think, but my shift didn't start until 4:30 PM, so I wasn't missing any money. He was!

It got to the point that his boss would call my cell phone to wake Javari up for work and say he would come and pick him up to make sure he made it to work. His boss was very caring and went the extra mile for Javari. You didn't see that in a lot of managers. Shoot, if you didn't come to work, that was you!

That only lasted for so long, after still not caring to go to work, even with the manager trying his best to motivate Javari, The company fired him. I did not know he was fired, either. He got paid on Friday and began to shower us with gifts and outings. He also was getting Tattoo's everyday for an entire week. The first one was our son's name on his back, T-I-Y-L-E-R written in huge letters on his back. Little did I know Javari was spending up all his money from his LAST check before being completely unemployed.

I found out in the upcoming week because he was just staying home all week. I asked him why he wasn't going to work, and this fool said the company was taking a break from work orders, but they were meeting this evening to review the details. I mean, he was very strategic with the lie he was telling me. He had me drive him to some building downtown near Kennedy and got out of the car, he went around the corner while me and the kids sat in the car for him.

About 30 minutes later, he came back and sat in the passenger seat with a blank look on his face. He never faced me when getting in the car; he just kept looking out the window. I immediately put my hand on his leg and asked if everything was okay out of concern.

"No, they just laid off everyone today, stating there is no more work right now," He said in a gloomy voice.

"Oh no, it's ok, you can get another Job, baby," I said

I was encouraging him, but inside, I knew why he lost his job. This could have been prevented. Now, ALL of the bills were going to be on me. Javari had to get a plan, and he needed to get a plan fast because one thing my granny taught me is never to take care of a man,

A few months have passed, and Jamie still doesn't have a job. He would only lay around all day and night and wasn't even applying for a job. He wouldn't even follow up with any jobs if he did apply. This annoyed and aggravated me, and I can't lie it also made me angry. I was a woman and a mother busting my butt to work and keep all the bills paid, and he was ok with not stepping up.

By now, TJ had turned one year old, and Tiyrel was 4.5. I had to make the hard decision to tell Javari he had to go. I just refused to let him lay up on me and not help me. My granny always said, "You can do bad by yourself!"So he moved out and went back to his mothers home, which was literally only five minutes away.

Once he moved, it was ironic that he landed a job at a local Hard Rock Casino in Tampa. I'm not really sure what type of work he was doing because since we didn't live together anymore, we didn't discuss these types of things.

While working overnights at the Hard Rock Casino, instead of focusing on his already-made family and becoming a better man, Javari meets a girl at the casino. They quickly begin to talk and ultimately start to date. Javari and I were not officially broken up, but we didn't live together. We actually had a plan to move back together once he became more stable.

While the lease ended at the apartment I lived at on 40th Street, I moved to an apartment community in Brandon called "Windermere Apartments."These were income, and my rent was only $464.00!! I had a great deal. So Javari moved back in with us, and he was working and things were going well again. We were even expecting our second child together, which was a girl, so we decided to name her Tiyrah. I was about six months pregnant. I was soon to be a mother of three.

One night, I was preparing dinner for us and there was a knock at the door. We had just moved to this apartment, so no one really knew where we were located. I was unsure who was on the other side of the door. Javari came out of the room "I will get it, baby,"and he answered the door. I didn't pay attention to him because I was still trying to complete our dinner. I noticed he had gone outside and shut the door.

So I called the boys and cleaned them up to get ready to eat. I sat them at their table, made plates, and then gave them food. I made Javari a plate, and he still was not back in the house, so I went to open the door. I had no idea what I was walking into when I opened the door.

There stood Javari and a tall caramel complexion skin girl. She was bigger than me. Then, on our stairs, there stood about six more girls. The Girl was standing there arguing with Javari about something. So I quickly interrupted them.

"Um, what the heck is going on here"? I stood there rubbing my stomach because Tiyrah began to move a lot. The girls on the stairs began to get in an uproar, screaming they were going to beat me up, etc. And the girl closer to us kept saying.

"Javari tell her, Javari tell her," she repeated.

Javari was still trying to calm all of them down and shielding me but demanding I go back in the house. I wasn't even listening to him. I was not going back in the house! Why were all these young girls standing at my door arguing and threatening to fight me? Since I was pregnant, I had to think about the safety of my daughter. However I was really ready to slap all these girls.

After a moment, no one could calm down and Javari opened our front door and pushed me inside since I wouldn't go willingly.

"GO IN THE HOUSE, ASH!" He screamed.

This time, I listened, and I went to check on the boys. They were peacefully eating and had no idea what was going on outside. Moments later, Javari walks in, rubbing his head and looking all stressed out! I needed answers this time; I wasn't letting any of this slide.

"Who was that Javari, and why did they come to our house"? I asked in a loud tone.

He came over to hug me, I wasn't in the mood for no hugs! I pushed him away and crossed my arms over my big belly. Tiyrah must have known I was mad because she was squirming every chance she got.

"Baby, during our little break, when I went back to my mom's, I ended up hooking up with this girl at my job.

"Hooking up"? What do you mean, Javari?

"We had sex. And now, even worse, she is pregnant now"He said that so fast, I had to hear that again to make sure I heard him right.

"She's pregnant"? I screamed. My heart began to race, my stomach began to hurt, and tears began to roll down my face. I sat down on the couch and just cried so hard.

"How could you do this to me, Javari, WHYYYY???

He stood there in shock, and not knowing what to do, he held me and repeatedly apologized for his actions. His sorry wasn't enough. Javari had got someone pregnant at the same time that I was pregnant. This was the most disrespectful thing I had experienced. I was so heartbroken. I felt like nothing. He ruined our family.

Now what???

Chapter 19: Fixing Me

After finding out that Javari had gotten another girl pregnant, I was devastated. I had become so broken. But I put him before myself. I didn't matter; my feelings didn't matter. I didn't want to lose my family. I also didn't want to fail in this relationship. I wanted my kids to have a dad and mom in the home.

I didn't want them to grow up the way I did. So, I decided to stick it out and try to make it work. I was going to stay with Javari, and we were going to figure out how we were going about his new baby on the outside of our home.

Those plans sounded good. He even proposed to me, I assume in hopes of making things better. I swear every day, I gave this relationship all I had. I couldn't lie; I had a huge resentment towards him.

Then, one morning, I wasn't feeling well at all. I would go to the bathroom, and I had a lot of irritation and pain down there. I didn't know what was going on. I noticed something different in the center of my panties. It was a yellow or neon-colored discharge. I was freaking out! What was this?

I immediately called my doctor to get her the earliest appointment. Lucky me, I was able to get in today. I went to the appointment and told her my symptoms. She asked if I was with any new partners. I told her no, only my boyfriend. She completed a pap smear & tested me for all these different types of STDs and said the results would be back tomorrow.

Dr. Williams promised she would give me a call. In the meantime, she supplied me with some antibiotics and ordered me to take all of them every day for the next two weeks.

I left that appointment feeling scared and anxious. I hope I didn't have an STD, especially while pregnant with my baby girl. I returned to the car and said a quick prayer to cover and protect me. When I went home. I told Javari what was wrong with me and that I would get the test results tomorrow. He even had the same colored discharge and never said anything to me. I demanded he get checked at the hospital ASAP!

He noticed something wrong with himself and didn't say anything about it. I went off about that because this was not only my life but my unborn baby girl's life he was playing with because he was always cheating! He even tried to play me as if I was some complete idiot, stating that nothing was wrong and that was the normal color of semen or discharge. I was disgusted! What was wrong with this boy? That night, we didn't speak for the rest of the night.

The following day, I was anxiously awaiting the call from the doctor. She promptly called at about 10:00 AM as promised. I answered quickly.

"Hey, Mrs. Montgomery, This is Dr. Williams, We have your results. Are you ready to discuss this? She asked

"Whew yes mam,"I said, taking a deep breath in/out. My palms were sweaty. I was anxious to hear the results.

"Okay, we tested you for a standard STD Panel, and the results that came back are that you tested positive for Gonorrhea and also positive for Chlamydia.

My heart immediately sank! Javari did not love me or his baby; he put us at risk, which could harm both of us.

"So what do I do from here, Dr. Williams? Can this be cured? Will my baby be ok?

"Well, to just educate you a bit, I already prescribed medication for both sexually transmitted diseases. You want to make sure your partner knows so that they get treated right away! You and your baby will be just fine. You need to make sure to take all your medication. I will schedule a follow-up visit in about two weeks. I am also going to send over some information packets via email for you to look over." Said Dr. Williams

"Thank You so much, Dr. Williams,"I said squeaky.

"No worries, Mrs. Montgomery. Listen, learn from this, everything will be fine. I promise. Let's just make sure this doesn't happen again."She said

"Yes, ma'am, " I said, and we ended the call.

I was so tired of Javari Cheating on me and lying to me, and now I was really fed up because he just didn't care! This was the last straw. It was time for me and Javari to part ways. I remember going back home and letting him know. I no longer wanted to be with him. I explained why and told him to get his things and figure out where to go. He began to plead with me and then dared

56

to tell me that I wouldn't leave him. I wasn't staying with him & definitely wasn't going to marry him!

He had to have bumped his head! I don't know where he was going to go, but he was going to get the heck out of my house. After arguing with himself for over an hour. He finally called his brother, who didn't live far from us to pick him up. That was the last that I had seen from him for a while. From that moment, I just focused on myself and the Kids. I continued to work and just came home and became a mom to my soon-to-be 3-pack.

A lot of the time, I would help my granny out at her home daycare when she needed me. Sometimes, she would have errands to run or doctor appointments, and I would watch the kids and fill in until she got back. While doing so, I was able to connect with all of the parents. They loved me there, and their kids became a part of our family. One day, my granny had to be someone, so she left me in charge.

This evening, I was watching a baby named Navaeh. She had to be about one year old, but she looked five or six months old. However, she was so tiny and cute. Her mom would often drop her off in the morning, and then her dad, Treece, would pick her up in the evening.

This one evening, Treece came to pick up his baby as usual, but today was different because my granny wasn't home. He began to make small talk and thanked me for watching his daughter and taking care of her. Of course, I didn't mind. I loved kids, and I also enjoyed helping my grandmother. After he gathered all of her belongings, he signed her out and then wrote his number on a piece of paper and handed it to me.

I looked confused and down at the paper. While I looked up at him, he said you should let me take you out sometime. He smiled. Treece was a very handsome

professional man. He was about 6'0 feet tall. He had a low-cut haircut and tapered facial hair. He had a caramel complexion, nice clear skin, and dressed really nicely.

Some days he had on nice suits, or jeans and a nice dress shirt. He was definitely eye candy and caught my eye. However, I never looked at him this way until today since he was showing me interest. This was weird. I was pregnant and full of baby at this point. I was giving birth in about 2 months or so. So there was confusion why this man was even talking to me.

"Wait, aren't you married?" I asked.

"Married?" He chuckled in disbelief.

"No, I'm not married. What made you think that?" he asked.

"Well, Nevaeh's mom always referred to you as her husband, so I assumed you were," I explained.

"No, we're not together. We're just roommates and good friends. We're co-parenting our daughter, that's all," he said.

"Oh, I wonder why she would say that," I replied.

He then gave me a hug and told me to call him later. I assured him I would and closed the door behind him. I never called him, though. I mean, I had too much going on. I was a single mother of three children, and I just wanted to fix myself. I had no time nor the energy to entertain anyone else. At this point, I was just over men. I stayed focused and ensured I was being the best for my children.

For the next few months, I'd occasionally see Treece, but with my heavy workload, our meetings were sparse. I kept his number and one day decided to text him. The message simply included my name and number. It seemed he had been waiting for me to reach out because he responded promptly! I didn't reply intentionally. With my baby on the way, I needed to focus on preparing for that."

I remember being at home alone during the day. My granny had the boys, of course, at the daycare. I was resting and then my back began to ache badly, and all these sharp pains started coming out of nowhere. I was having Braxton Hicks kicks these past few weeks, but they were all false alarms.

Every time I went to the hospital, they would send me home because I was not going into labor. I was just tired of being pregnant at this point. I wanted to have her NOW. Not to mention I was all alone going through this again.

The pain would not slow down or stop, so I packed my bag and got in my car to drive myself to the hospital. I called my granny and my mom to let them know what was going on. My mom was working, so she said she would meet me at the hospital when she got off work. My granny had to close the daycare and would head over after that.

I attempted to call Javari to let him know what was going on, but he didn't answer, so I left a voicemail and also sent a text.

As I began to drive, the pain strikes were getting closer together and more painful. I was having Contractions. This seemed to be the real thing because I had to pull over. I couldn't drive myself. I called 9-1-1 from my cell phone number.

911 What's your emergency? Asked the operator

"Yes, I'm Ashley Montgomery, and I'm pregnant and about to have my baby on the side of the road. I need help,"I said.

The operator began to ask me questions and make sure I was safe. Before I knew it, an ambulance fire truck and police cars pulled behind me. They rushed over to me and placed me in the back of the ambulance to check my vitals. The paramedics at that time confirmed that I was having contractions and needed to get to the hospital immediately.

One of the police officers parked my car on the side of the road and then brought me my keys, and they rushed me to Tampa General Hospital. My aunt Carletta was in town from Cocoa Beach, FL, so she met me at the hospital. She was a great help. This was my biological father's sister. She loved me and my brother and always did her best to be a part of our lives. There was nothing she wouldn't do for us. I looked a lot like her, and our attitudes were the same.

As we arrived at the hospital, the paramedic team wheeled me to the labor and delivery area. I went straight in. The nurses grabbed a chart and began to ask me for information. Then a nurse came inside to check to see if I had dilated, and I was already 5 cm dilated. I was going to have my daughter today. My aunt was right by my side. I was so happy she was there with me. My mom was on her way from work. She had made it just in the nick of time because when she walked through the door on the phone, I was standing up in excruciating pain.

There wasn't enough time for pain meds or an epidural, so I was in excruciating pain and terrified. I was facing the daunting task of giving birth naturally! My mom had to cancel her choir rehearsal and her phone kept ringing non-stop while she was in the room.

"Yeah, girl, my daughter's in here about to have a baby, so choir rehearsal is canceled tonight," she explained over the phone.

She stayed on the call a bit longer until I screamed in agony, and she hurriedly ended the conversation. My aunt was beside me, rubbing my back and coaching me to breathe in and out.

My mom rushed over, comforting me and offering ice chips for my dry lips. She even brought chapstick to help soothe them. Quickly, she went to fetch the doctor as Tiyrah's head began to crown. The doctor and nurses hurried in, readying me for pushing.

After just 3-4 strong pushes, I heard the cries of my beautiful baby girl. She was perfect.

I had given birth to a precious princess named Tiyrah, weighing 8 pounds, 9 ounces, and measuring 22 inches long. She was a big baby! From the start, I vowed to shield her from any pain I had endured and to make sure she knew her worth.

She didn't need to endure pain before feeling loved. She became my purpose, a realization that dawned on me unexpectedly but profoundly.

I tried calling Javari repeatedly on the hospital phone, but there was no answer. I left a final message. He knew my due date, so he should have been there. However, he had moved on with Jayla after our breakup. She had even rented an apartment near Fletcher Ave and Bruce B Downs in some apartments called "Eagles Pointe."

She left her mom's house, and he moved in with her. I figured he went straight from my place to hers. Jessica and I had been arguing for so long that we were both worn out. We eventually became friends and started talking more. It became clear to us that Javari was playing both sides.

A few days after Tiyrah was born, I told Jessica about her. She informed Javari, and he came to see her.

Tiyrah had light skin, just like Javari's mom, Mrs. Polly. She looked

just like a baby doll. We were trying our best to co-parent, but Javari was dropping the ball in helping me with the kids. So, I had to make a hard choice to apply for child support. At the point that I did that, they asked for DNA for both of the kids. I completed this at the local Child support office, and we both received the results for both children about a month after.

I already knew the results, but to clear up any confusion or background conversations about Javari being the father of my children. The results read that both of our kids were 99.999999999% his. He claimed he already knew this too, however, it was clear in black and white now. After the birth of our daughter, Javari and I still would connect and ended up fooling around a few times. I knew it was wrong, but I was still so emotional, and this was the father of both of my children. It felt like I wasn't wrong and wanted my family.

I soon had to end all interactions between me and him because Jessica was my friend and she really thought they had a good relationship. I didn't want to hurt her. I was trying to tell her but she didn't want to listen. She found out for herself that Javari was no good. She gave birth to a baby girl in August. Her name was jaylani. She wasn't getting any financial help either, so she had to apply for child support, too, because they soon broke up, and he was no longer an active father for either of our kids.

Over the next three months, I focused solely on being the best mother I could to my children, regardless of what Javari wasn't doing. One afternoon, as I sat on the porch, my phone started ringing. It was TREECE! He was persistent. I decided to pick up.

"Hello?" I answered.

"Hey!" TREECE greeted enthusiastically.

"Hey, how are you?" I replied.

"I'm good. I've been trying to get in touch with you. Did you have the baby yet?"

"Yes, I did. I'm sorry I've been so busy. She's been keeping me occupied for about four months now!

"I bet, well send me some pictures, and do you need anything"?

"Ummm, no, not really."

"Okay, well, I still want to take you out. Would you be down for me to take you to breakfast tomorrow?

I was on the fence about Treece taking me out, but he insisted, and he wouldn't leave me alone until I accepted. So I agreed to him taking me out for breakfast the next morning. It was a Saturday. My mom was keeping the kids for a few for me, so this worked out. I told him to come and get me at 10:00 AM . He agreed, and we both hung up the phone.

That next morning, I got up and started to get ready for our morning date. I picked out a nice summer dress and some cute clear slides to match. I lotioned myself all over and sprayed my favorite body mist on. It was a Victoria's Secret Brand, and smelled like Sunflowers.

It was about 9:45, and I heard a knock at the door. I asked who it was, and of course it was Treece! He was early. When I opened the door, he greeted me with a bouquet of flowers. They were beautiful. I grabbed the flowers, and Treece leaned in to hug me. I closed the door behind me, and we walked down the stairs to his car. Treece was crazy about his car. He had a 2009 Dodge Charger. It was so classy. It was Black with nice chrome rims, chrome door handles and all. It was really nice. He opened the door for me, and I sat down. As he closed the door behind me, I thought he was really nice.

We made it to the restaurant (Denny's) and ordered our food. We ate and enjoyed a great conversation. I shared my status with Javari and everyone else. He told me he had finally found his own place and was no longer a roommate with anyone. We had a great morning. After we left the restaurant, he took me to the store to buy things for the baby. He had me pick out anything I wanted for her. I had a few things, and then he told me to ensure she had everything.

We left that store with a cart full of miscellaneous baby items. I was very grateful, but I still didn't know why he was doing all of this. He took me home and helped me take out all of the things he bought for Tiyrah. I thanked him again, and he hugged me before going on his way.

I enjoyed that day with him, and he seemed to be a nice guy. Shortly after there was a knock at the door. I opened the door, and it was the kids. My mom was dropping them off, She never kept them for long, was too young to be anybody's grandma, and had a life to live, I guess. I brought them into the house and played with them for a while. Tiyrel was the oldest, and he was a little man, you couldn't tell this boy he wasn't his sibling's daddy.

After connecting that day, Treece would call and message me daily and make sure I and the kids were well. Our relationship accelerated pretty fast. I fell for him fast. He would always wine and dine me and the kids. He was twelve years older than me, though. He often said my age didn't matter because I was very mature. I met him when I was eighteen but didn't start to talk to him until I was twenty years old.

We finally made it official, I finally told him how I felt about him and was truly in love. This is when all hell broke loose. Treece would often spend the night over at my house. Noticed I could never go to his house. So I asked to go over to his place. He would give a million excuses. Then, the visits to me even slowed down. Treece stopped answering the phone or texting back promptly. Something was going on, and something was different.

He did give me his address, and I went over, which was about 35 minutes away from Brandon. His place was a nice one-bedroom condo. He was a very clean man. His taste in furniture and decorating was immaculate, too. I spent the night that night and didn't go home until the next morning. He left his key and told me to leave it under the mat. When I woke up, I actually went and made a copy of the key because something was not right with Treece, and I was going to find out.

My grandmother found out that we were together and didn't like the idea of the jump, she said his mother often talked about how he was such a womanizer and a liar, etc. She warned me to leave him alone and not fall for his tricks. I, on the other hand, just thought my granny was being hard on me. I wish I knew that warning came before destruction.

In the weeks ahead, I discovered I was pregnant again. I shared the news with Treece, but his response shattered me—he wasn't ready for another baby. Nevaeh was already a few years old, and Tiyrah wasn't even a year yet. I didn't feel prepared either. Reluctantly, Treece suggested I get an abortion since our circumstances weren't ideal.

I was terrified but felt compelled to agree, caught up in my feelings for him. One morning, he drove me to an abortion clinic on Fletcher Ave, a purple brick building surrounded by protesters with signs. He dropped me off, promising to return later.

As I walked inside, the protesters pleaded with me not to enter this building and to choose life. I had to tune them out because they almost made

As I stepped inside, protesters begged me not to go in, urging me to choose life. Their pleas nearly made me reconsider, but it was too late to turn back now.

Treece had already driven away, and I knew he'd leave me if I didn't go through with it. This would be one of the hardest decisions I have ever made in my entire life.

Jeremiah 1:5: *Before I formed you in the womb I knew you, before you were born I set you apart; I appointed you as a prophet to the nations."*

CHAPTER 20: LIFE IS OVER

I made it inside the building and walked up to the front counter. A familiar face greeted me. Oh my God, this was the last thing I needed to be noticed by someone I knew at an abortion clinic. It was my cousin's old neighbor. However, she was really nice. She didn't make things awkward, and she just acted normal, which made my heart at ease. She handed me a clipboard with paperwork and asked me to complete the forms.

I went to have a seat to complete them. Once I had completed all the forms, I returned them to the front desk. I then paid her $500.00 cash. I was asked to have a seat, and they would call me back when they were ready. Not long after sitting. A tall lady with blonde hair called my name. I stood up and followed her. She took me to a room with a couch against the wall, a computer desk, and another office chair. She asked me to sit on the couch, and she sat at her desk.

The reason why we were in this office, she wanted to make sure that having this abortion was my decision and something that I really wanted to do. She asked me a series of questions to verify if I qualified to get the abortion completed today. I made sure not to say I wasn't sure because they wouldn't let me do this. After I was done, I was walked to a medical room, with a chair you would usually have a pap smear in. There was also this huge machine that looked like a generator.

There was also an oxygen tank and mask in the same corner. Next to the medical chair, there was a table full of different medical tools. This scared me! I was really about to let a doctor kill my baby. I was so in love with Treece by now that nothing could change my mind. Shortly after a doctor and I assume his nurse assistant was the young lady with him. The young lady completed an ultrasound on me. She confirmed with the doctor I was 9 weeks pregnant.

The doctor said Hello and was straight to the point. He grabbed the mask from out the corner and then asked me to count down from 10. As I count down, I see the assistant turning on the machine I thought was the generator. I think this was the machine they got rid of the baby in. When I got to number seven I don't remember anything else after that. I was as fast asleep, My eyes were completely shut. The next time I opened my eyes, I was in a room full of blue recliner chairs, that were sectioned off by curtains. The room was extremely cold and gave off a stitch of a stale smell. I was covered in a thin tan colored blanket.

I felt so sleepy and had a sort of high feeling. I looked around and other women were sitting in the same recliner as me. We all were bundled in these tan blankets. Finally, my memory began to come in, I remembered what I had seen before I went to sleep. Then it hit me: I had an abortion, I was a murderer. I killed my baby! Now, I was beginning to regret this decision, but now it was all too late. The tears began to roll down my face. I felt so low and sad and full of regret!

As I began to wipe my face using the blanket, the nurse assistant came over to tell me my ride was here to pick me up. She helped me in a wheelchair and gathered my things. She pushed me to a side of the building with an exit door. Treece was standing at the door. His car was pulled up to the door. He grabbed my things from the nurse's assistant and helped me in the car. I sat in silence the entire ride home. Treece was quiet, too, but he finally asked me if I was hungry. I said I was, so he stopped by McDonald's for food.

I really had no appetite, at this point, I became numb. I felt lifeless. After he got the food for me, he pulled into my apartment complex. He helped me up the stairs and got me settled in. Not even 10 minutes later, he said he had to go. I sat there looking dumb. This man was really leaving me alone after having an abortion? He clearly was showing me he didn't even care. So, as he left, I just sat in bed all alone, crying. My heart was aching so badly. I had never felt so much emotional pain in my life! I screamed, "WHY"!!!!!! Loudly. After crying for hours, it left me exhausted.

I ended up falling asleep, awakened by my cell phone ringing. It was my mom, she was letting me know she was on her way to bring my kids home. I just said ok, but I was in no shape to be around anyone. I just wanted to stay locked up in my room alone. I must have dozed off again because I was startled by a knock at the door. I could hear the kids calling me "Mommy"through the door. My stomach was hurting, so I walked slowly to the door.

I opened the door, and my mom and kids walked in. All the kids ran to me, hugging me. Tiyrah was still a baby, so she reached up for me to pick her up. I picked her up and gave all of them kisses and hugs. My mom noticed something was off with my demeanor.

"Are you ok?"she asked.

"Yes,"I answered quickly to brush her off. Inside, I was so broken down. I was so depressed, and now I felt like I wanted to kill myself. There was really no reason for me to live. Treece had abandoned me when I needed him the most.

I felt used and abused. How could he say he loved me and treat me like this? He left me in my apartment in the worst shape ever!

My mom made sure the kids were good and then she left. For the rest of the night, I stayed locked in my room. I wasn't attentive to the kids. I was in a dark place. Tiyrel was the oldest; he was about six years old and doing what he could for the kids. I wasn't in my right mind, I know it sounds terrible but I didn't even care what they needed or not. I just wanted life to be over.

Luckily, my mom came over the next morning, and the kids opened the door. I was still locked in my room in the dark. I didn't get any calls from Treece, no messages or anything. This made me fall into a deep level of depression and feeling worthless. I could hear my mom banging on the other side of the door. Screaming at me to open my bedroom door. I could hear her asking Tiyrel when was the last time they ate.

I got up and answered the door, it was pitch black in the room. My blinds were closed, and my dark black curtains were down, blocking out the sun. She immediately began yelling at me. What is wrong with you, Ash? These kids haven't eaten since I left, and you are closed up in the dark. I just stood there. I couldn't even speak. I slid down my bedroom floor and just sat against the wall.

At this point, my mom was going in on me, but I wasn't responding, so she knew something was really wrong. She then got the kids dressed and the baby bag packed and said she was taking them with her. She wasn't going to leave them with me in the condition that I was in. I was relieved but I still felt so empty. My mom had no idea what I was battling. I got up to grab my phone. I began to text Treece.

Text Read: "Hey, why are you ignoring me? Please call me. I love you." I hit send nervously. I waited hours for a response. The hours turned into days. I didn't hear from Treece until two weeks later!

He texted me out of the blue. "Good Morning Beautiful"like he just didn't disappear for fifteen days, like he did not abandon me after having an abortion! This was very hurtful and upsetting. Truth be told when I saw his name on my phone, I lit up like a light bulb, just like an idiot. I quickly texted back, asking where he was and why he wasn't responding to me.

The excuse he gave was that he lost his phone and he was just able to get a new one. I should have known better and at this point, this should have been the end of me and Treece's relationship and interaction. Sadly, it wasn't, it was just the beginning of our love story or our love spell full of toxicity.

After talking for a while Treece asked to come over because he missed me. I fell for the trap and allowed him to come. Every time he came, he would help me with the kids and settle them. Tiyrah was a baby and slept in my room, so you often found Treece holding and talking to her. I smiled as I watched him with her. He was always a great dad to his daughter Navaeh, so the care he showed Tiyrah was the same. I wanted all my kids to have a man in their life like Treece. and, of course, a father. All they had was me.

Treece stayed over that night and got up for work early the next morning. The night felt like I was in heaven. He was always so soft, sensual, and attentive. He gave me a nice full body massage, he ordered us food and we watched a movie until both of us fell asRoycep cuddled up. He apologized for not trying to reach out in two weeks. Honestly, I knew he was lying, but I didn't care because I was lost in all the lust that I thought was love.

Treece began to come over more often for the next month or so. Around this time, we pretty much became a couple. He had his own place on the water past the Oldsmar area, and I would stay over there sometimes when my granny kept the kids. I soon found out I was expecting yet ANOTHER baby. This time, I was NOT aborting our child.

I told Treece and showed him the test, he promised to be here for me. I made it clear that this baby was here to stay. I didn't want to go through the trauma again of having an abortion. He agreed, and he promised not to leave my side this time. He did keep his word, but soon, I would find myself being so far away from him.

Treece worked for Chase Bank and had just received a proportion. I remember it was Father's Day weekend, so I wanted to do something special for him. I was cooking dinner for him and just wanted to make this weekend all about him. As I sat on the couch, I got a text from a friend who worked downtown then.

The text read: Hey Ash, what's your baby daddy's name again?

This was so random, plus at this time, I had a total of three, so I responded......

"Ummmmm which one"?

"The one you are pregnant by now,"she said.

"His name is Treece, why what's up"?

"I'm going to send you some stuff in your email. Now I'm just full of anxiety. What was this girl about to send to my email???

I checked my email while Treece was busy watching TV. It was a large file, but the paperwork basically showed that Treece was in the courts for not one but two paternity cases! I was hurt, and my heart sunk! "Did Treece have more kids?" I only knew Treece had one child, Navaeh, the baby my grandmother kept at her daycare.

Treece walks into the room to check in on me, and I just close the computer. I don't want him to suspect anything. I stand up and give him a hug. After I make his plate, I am going to ask him about this.

I had made our plates, and we were done. We were enjoying sitting next to each other on the couch and listening to music.All I was thinking about was that email my friend had just sent me. I began to rub the back of his head, gently massaging it.

"Baby, can I ask you something?"I asked

"Yes, anything, baby," he said

"How many kids do you have ?"

"What baby"? He asked while looking up at me, confused.

"How many kids do you have, "I asked sternly!

"I have four kids, baby."Dominique, Le'treece Jr., Le'Tron, and Nevaeh. My other kids are a little older. I had my first son when I was sixteen and the next two from my ex-wife. Last, you know Navaeh is from Jane. You met her already.

I sat there silently because I was happy he told part of the truth. There were two other children that he didn't mention. Their birthdays were in 2008 and 2009. It was 2010 now, so they were a little close in age. I couldn't really see if they had the same mother or not.

"Are you sure that is all, baby?"I asked

He laughed before answering. "Yes, I'm sure!"

I left it alone. I will soon get to the bottom of this. I was only twenty years old and naive sometimes, but that didn't mean I was dumb. Treece then wanted some dessert. He had a taste for some ice cream and cake. I offered to run to Publix quickly to get the items. I was trying to be generous with it being Father's Day weekend. I ran to the room to get my shoes, and I left for the store.

I told Treece I would be right back, and I closed the door. It didn't take me long to run to the store, Publix was only five minutes away. So I got back quickly. When I arrived back, I unlocked the door and walked in with a bag of treats.

"Baby, I have your cake and ice cream!"I screeched excitedly. I could hear the TV still on, but he didn't answer me. I walked toward the living room, and Treece wasn't there or on the couch. I thought maybe he was in the bathroom. So I walked towards my bedroom.

I called his name, but there was no answer and no Treece in sight. This was pretty weird. He may have gone to the store or something? But why didn't he just go with me if he needed anything? I grabbed my cell phone out of my purse and called him immediately. The cell phone began to just pick up on the first ring. I called several more times and still no answer. I began to get nervous. Hours passed and I still didn't hear from Treece. By this time, I had called all the hospitals and the jails. Treece was nowhere to be found. My emotion now turned into anger.

Treece was notorious for disappearing acts, but did this dude really have the audacity to do this to me now and today out of all days? I grabbed my keys and decided to drive to his house. I pulled up, and to my surprise, his car wasn't parked in the parking lot. The next thing I noticed was that his blinds were up in his living room. I parked my car and got out. I walked to the front door and peeked through the window.

I couldn't believe what I had seen, Treece's apartment was completely empty! I was able to walk to the side of the apartment where his bedroom window was, and the blinds were pulled up there as well, and there was nothing in sight. All the furniture, EVERYTHING WAS GONE! I ran back to my car with tears running down my face. Treece had moved and didn't even tell me, and now he disappeared and was not answering his phone. I hated when he did this to me.

I called his phone for hours, and no pickup and no response to my text messages. Then suddenly, it started to pick up on the first ring, leading me to his voicemail. I had become a total wreck. I went back home, and I couldn't sleep. I was a whole mess. I had a migraine and was completely stressed out. I called my granny and asked if it was ok that the kids stayed over that night because I was just so tired. She agreed because they went to her daycare anyway.

The next day, I woke up and there was nothing from Treece still. So now I was beyond worried. I decided to go over to his mom's house. I grabbed some breakfast first and then headed out. When I arrived, I knocked on the door. His mother was a very light-skinned lady, kind of short, had medium-length hair that was pulled back, and average size weight. She wore glasses and was surprised to see me. I didn't call before I came. I was in so much shock I just rushed over without even thinking. When she opened the door. I explained what was going on and that I needed help.

She let me in and asked if I was okay. I gave her a look that said it all: I was emotionally drained. I don't know why Treece continued to do this to me. So his mother said she would call from her phone.She claimed to have talked to him a few days ago but had not heard anything since. She took her cell phone out and dialed Treece. The phone began to ring.

"Hey ma,"Treece answered

"Hey, son, How are you? "replied his mom

Now I am pissed! Nothing was wrong with him and he was ignoring all my calls and just disappeared from the house with no explanation!

"Well, I have Ashley sitting here with me, and she has been looking for you, she is pregnant and worried Treece"

"oh no, I'm sorry she is worried, I had a flight I had to catch, and my phone died and had no charger until now,"

"I'm going to give her the phone,"she said and she passed me the phone.

I took the phone outside and on the front porch for privacy. I felt so dumb.

"Treece, where the hell are you "? I yelled

71

"Baby, calm down, I'm in Texas"!

"You are in TEXAS!"What are you doing in Texas Treece"?

"Well, I didn't know how to tell you this, and I didn't want you to be mad, but I moved here for a position at work."

"Why didn't you tell me"? Why did you just leave me like that?"I was calling and blowing up your phone.

I began to cry, I was so emotional these days, every little thing bothered me. This was not right, though. Treece didn't care for anyone else's feelings but his own.

"Baby, I'm sorry. I didn't mean to hurt you, but I knew you would be crying, so I just thought about leaving.

"That's so dumb, I'm crying now, so what did you accomplish"? Nothing!

I hung up the phone before he could answer, and I walked over and handed his mother the phone. She stopped to hug me and said that everything would be okay and that I should call her if I needed anything.

I agreed and rushed out the door. From that point, I decided to ignore Treece just like he did me, he wouldn't like it if I gave him a taste of his own medicine! I was in Tampa with almost 4 kids, and he was all the way in Texas and didn't even tell me. This was so foolish!

I looked at the clock, and it was 9:45 AM. I had to be at work at 11:00 AM., so I rushed home to get dressed. After I was fully dressed and ready for work, I went in. I worked for United Health Care. It was a customer service position. My shift was 11 a.m.- 8 p.m. So, by the time I got off, the kids were always sleeping.

On my way to work, the car was driving a little funny. The oil light had come on, but it was too late to stop now, so I got it in the morning. The next morning before work, I was driving to the auto part store so I could get the oil. That's when the car began to ride really rough and started making a loud crashing sound.

I pulled into the gas station, grabbed some oil, and put it in the car. I turned the car back on, and it was still making all this noise. I decided to drive up the street a little, and it was still riding rough, just like before.

Then, out of nowhere, the car began to slow down and just shut off. I tried restarting it, and it would not budge. Omg I didn't need this today. I had to be at work. I had already been late a few times, and they had already given me a warning saying I could only be late two more times or I would be let go. I immediately called my friend Denise because she worked with me. I asked her if she could give me a ride. She said sure, but the bad thing was she wasn't able to take me home.

My grandmother then started keeping the kids Monday-Friday night and day for me, because I didn't have a car to commute to get the kids. Also, my shift was midday so it didn't make sense to be doing all that driving back and forth. I was so sad my car wasn't working. However, a mechanic was going to let me know what was wrong with it in the morning.

That next morning, I woke up to the mechanic asking me to meet him at the gas station where the car had stalled on me. It wasn't too far from my apartment so I brushed my teeth and washed my face, and I began to walk to the gas station. When I arrived, the mechanic was waiting for me. He grabbed a machine, put the keys in the ignition, and started the car. When he turned on the car and heard the sound, he looked worried.

"Oh no,"he said

"Oh no,"? I repeated

"Little lady, the engine is gone in the car. You are better off getting a new car than getting it fixed."

"Omg, no,"I said loudly. This was the last thing that I needed right now. Treece was in Texas, my grandma had the kids full time trying to help me, I was pregnant and tired, and I only had one more strike at work, and I was out the door!

The mechanic apologized, and then he said to me he would tow me back to my house. I hopped in his truck, he connected my car to the back of his and he rode me home. Now I was a carless pregnant mother of four and NO VEHICLE, and hanging on like a thread to my current job. What else could go WRONG???????

Chapter 21- Unexpected Blessings & Surprises

Have you ever felt like your life was a constant storm of turmoil and chaos? It's like everything is collapsing around you. The hardest part is thinking it can't possibly get worse, but somehow it always does. That's exactly where I found myself at this moment.

What else could possibly go wrong now? Why couldn't I just catch a break?

My life felt like it was falling apart. Frustration and disbelief gripped me as I faced the consequences of those eight minutes. Losing my job was a harsh blow, especially because I had tried to do the right thing by showing up despite the odds. Now, uncertainty loomed over me like a dark cloud. How was I going to make ends meet without a job? It seemed like every effort to stabilize my life was met with another setback.

As I reflected on the situation, I couldn't help but feel betrayed by the circumstances. One moment of lateness, compounded by factors beyond my control, had unraveled months of hard work and dedication. It was a stark reminder of how fragile stability can be in the face of unexpected challenges.

Here's how it happened. After a couple of hours at work, I thought I had dodged another bullet for being late yet again. But just before my break, a team lead, Richard, called me into his office. Wanting to be prepared, I asked if I needed anything. He assured me I didn't and said I'd be back on the phone soon. My nerves eased since Richard and I had a good rapport. He was a tall, easygoing guy in his early forties, always friendly and funny.

He led me to a small office space with a desk and two chairs in it. There was already someone waiting for me to arrive. It was a short white lady with sandy-red pepper-colored curly hair. She smiled as I entered the room and asked me to have a seat. Richard closed the door behind him, and then we began to talk.

"Hi Ashley, My name is Beth, I am the Human Resources Director Beth"

"Hi, Mrs. Beth,"

"How is everything going? How are you enjoying your role here at United Health Care"?

"I love it, everything is going well! I replied

"Awesome,well, we are glad that things are going well for you, unfortunately, we have to have a very uncomfortable conversation today.

Beth then pulled out a paper with my name on it. She began to explain that my attendance had not been that great during the period of time that I had been with the company. She pointed to each date listed on the sheet, identifying each day I had called out of work or been late. I sat there quietly because I was scared of what she was going to say next.

Then, the worst that I thought could happen did happen.

"So I'm afraid, Ashley, that today will be your last day here at United Health Care"

I simply said "okay," stood up, and opened the door. Richard and another man were waiting outside with a box containing all my belongings from my desk. It felt humiliating to be escorted out like this. I wanted to check if they had cleared everything from my desk, but they stopped me from going back. They assured me everything was in the box.

I couldn't believe they were letting me go like this. I was embarrassed and ashamed, but I tried not to show it. Acting unfazed, I took the box and walked out. Once outside, I sifted through it to find what I needed. I kept only my notebook, phone, and charger.

I didn't have a car, so I was stuck & stranded. How was I going to get home? I lived only eleven minutes away but it was a long way to walk. I had no other choice but to begin walking. I had little money and no other options. I threw the brown cardboard box in the bushes and didn't look back.

The weather was scorching hot and unbearable. Adding to my discomfort, I was pregnant and already struggling to catch my breath. After walking about two miles, I stopped at a coffee shop in a nearby plaza and dialed a yellow cab from my phone. Walking further wasn't an option. Within moments, the cab arrived, pulling into my apartment complex in under three minutes.

I handed the driver a $10 bill, thanked him, and stepped out of the car.

I entered the house and collapsed onto the bed, utterly exhausted and in need of rest. After a short while, I got up to grab a bottle of water and called my granny to let her know I was home. I suggested she could bring the kids over whenever she was ready. Luckily, she wasn't in a rush, which gave me much-needed alone time to gather my thoughts.

In the living room, I turned on the television and fetched my laptop. Without hesitation, I began my job search on careerbuilder.com, a website for finding local job openings. Being a single mother, I couldn't afford to stay unemployed. I found a customer service position with Alltel Wireless and swiftly uploaded my resume and completed the application.

After finishing a few more job applications and surveys, I decided to text Treece. I couldn't bring myself to admit I'd lost my job. I always felt I had to present my best self to him. He was so professional and put together, and I felt I needed to match that image. I kept the struggles hidden because I felt inadequate compared to him. I thought I was lucky he even wanted to talk to me.

I can't explain why I felt this way. I never understood why a man twelve years older than me would be interested. I was much younger, still trying to find my way, while he seemed so established. I was often reckless and inexperienced, whereas he was smart and responsible. We were complete opposites at that point in our lives.

I guess none of that really mattered now. I was about to give birth to his son. We found out we were having a baby boy and decided to name him Le'Tory. I was eager to have him. I always struggled with the final stretch of pregnancy. It felt like it would never end.

After sending a greeting, Treece called me.

"Hello?" I answered.

"Hey baby, how are you feeling?" he asked.

I took a deep breath and replied, "Tired as usual."

"When are you coming home? The baby will be here next month, and I could really use your help."

"Baby, I will be home next month. We have the maternity photoshoot scheduled, remember?"he asked

Baby, I'll be home next month. Remember we have the maternity photoshoot scheduled?" he asked.

I had forgotten about the photoshoot we planned. Last time Treece was in town, we spotted a studio called "Picture Perfect" at Brandon Mall. We set up an appointment for a few weeks later, giving us time to pick outfits and plan my hairstyle.

I was excited but also missed Treece dearly. I couldn't wait to see him. Yet, I couldn't shake the thought of what he might be doing in Texas. Treece was handsome but had trouble saying no to women. Being in Florida, I doubted he was alone all this time waiting for me. His lack of self-control and respect troubled me, not just for us but for himself and other women.

After chatting a bit longer, I told him I'd call him later. Exhausted from the day, I fell asleep on the living room couch and slept through until morning.

My phone rang, showing an unfamiliar number. Despite that, I answered.

"Hello?"

"Hi, I'm trying to reach Ashley, please," a woman's soft voice came through the line.

"Yes, ma'am, this is Ashley. How can I help you?"

"I'm Evelyn from Alltel Wireless. I'm calling because you applied for a customer service role with us."

"Oh yes, ma'am, I did just yesterday," I replied.

"Yes, you sure did. We were impressed with your resume and wanted to see if you are available today to complete an interview."

"Yes, I sure can. What is your availability?"If possible, we can connect today at 1 p.m".

'1:00 PM is available and a great time. So we will connect then. Talk to you soon.

"Great, thanks! I replied.

I couldn't believe how quickly they called about the job. I was determined to ace that interview like I always did. I'm confident in my speaking skills and interview abilities. After hanging up, I prepared myself for later by taking a shower.

Moments after drying off, the phone rang again, and I hurried to answer. Something felt off; my usually lively mom was silent. Her quiet weeping worried me.

She continued to cry so hard that her words were barely understandable. I was deeply concerned but knew I had to stay strong for her. Seeing her break down like this was alarming because she was always the pillar of strength in our family.

After she calmed down a bit, she told me that she had been laid off from her job at Florida Orthopaedic Institute today. She was devastated and felt betrayed after working there for fourteen years. Hearing her pain resonated with me deeply, especially since I had just lost my job too. It was a sudden blow, leaving us both unsure of what the future held with our incomes unexpectedly cut off.

Being the problem solver I am, I immediately went into action mode. I assured my mom that I would help her find a new job once she got home, without mentioning that I had lost my own job the day before. Keeping it a secret was crucial for now, as I was confident I would secure a new job quickly. In all my previous interviews, I had excelled and been hired on the spot. My priority now was helping my mom regain her stability.

After reassuring my mom, I focused on preparing for my interview. I ended the call and called for a cab to take me to the interview. Meeting with the recruiter and management made me a bit nervous; the interview felt more like an interrogation. The recruiter was direct and no-nonsense, leaving me uncertain about how well I had answered their questions. Their expressions gave away nothing about their impression of me

I had to be honest. This was the first time that I questioned whether I was going to get the job or not. After leaving the interview, I was told they would reach out to me soon. I already thought the worst and assumed they were not going to call me anyway. You know employers would say this just to get you out of their face and onto the next applicant.

I called another cab to pick me up, but to take me to my grandmother's house this time. She had the kids, and I wanted to get them and head home. I pulled up, and to my surprise, my mother was there. I was happy to see her. She looked so broken down. Her face was full of worry. It looked like she had been crying all day. I sat at the other end of my grandmother's table. She then began to tell me what happened at work.

Some of her co-workers had lied to management. They were mad at her for not approving some vacation time. They then all went to management, double-teaming her. Ultimately, management believed the other co-workers, and she was then let go.

I began to tell my mom not to worry that she would get another Job. I knew that was easier said than done. As I was trying to encourage her, we both were in the same boat. She ended up being unemployed for almost two months. She did get approved for unemployment, but it wasn't enough to pay all of her bills on her own. I know Ernesto was working, but he was working out of town. I didn't know what was going on with him assisting her, she didn't say much about it.

All I know is that she was about to drown in bills, so I offered to leave my apartment lease and move in with her. Her house was over 3000 sq feet, so she had enough room for all of us. I wanted to help her with her bills so she could rest and look for a job with less stress or weight on her shoulders.

Thankfully, she found a job at a nearby hospital and swiftly regained her position in management. I was proud and genuinely happy for her, and her excitement was palpable. But the joyous moment didn't endure. Unbeknownst to us, she couldn't cover her rent due to insufficient funds and lack of support from her husband. By the time she got a job and I moved in with her, it was too late. This unfortunate chain of events led to her eviction from the rented home. My brother, uncle, and grandparents stepped in to help move all her belongings into storage.

We all stayed with my grandparents until we could find our own places again. I was nearing my due date with my seven-month-old baby. During this time, I hadn't seen Treece in person for months. I had already begun my job at Alltel Wireless after getting hired. Eventually, Treece bought me a ticket to visit him in Texas.

I visited him for a week. It was a welcomed break from the kids and work. Treece was staying at his god-sister's newly built home that they hadn't moved into yet, so he stayed there temporarily. It was a beautiful two-story brick house. He was very attentive during my visit. He gave me tours, made breakfast, took me to movies and shopping. Overall, I had a great time.

But the joy was short-lived, and those seven days flew by. It was time for me to head back home to my babies. Treece dropped me off at the airport, gave me a hug, and asked me to call him once I landed. I was sad to leave, standing there, not wanting to go, wishing we could be together as a family where he was.

Treece noticed my sadness and suggested we move there with him, which briefly eased my mind. Despite feeling the baby squirm inside me, I composed myself and boarded the plane. The flight was short. When I arrived at Tampa International Airport, my mom picked me up, sensing something was wrong. She kept asking every ten minutes during the drive home.

Returning felt daunting. Back at my grandmother's house, there was always something happening. Still, seeing my kids again lifted my spirits.

Finally, we pulled into the front yard. As I opened the door, the kids rushed to greet me with hugs, kisses, and endless questions. They were fascinated by my plane trip since it was their first time hearing about it. Exhausted as I was, I answered all their questions, and we spent the evening eating and watching a movie before we all fell asleep.

The next morning, I grabbed my phone, surprised that Treece hadn't called to check if I was safe or okay. I was eight months pregnant with our son. The nerve of him! I was furious. As I started dialing his number, he sent a text:

"Good Morning Beautiful"

I couldn't believe it! How dare he act like everything was okay! I threw the phone on the floor in frustration. Moments later, it vibrated again. I thought it was him texting back, but it was a Facebook notification. I opened it and saw a message from someone I didn't know. It read:

"Hey Ashley! Me and you have so much in common."

I sat there, wondering what this unfamiliar person could have in common with me. Curious, I clicked on the profile link, and the image that appeared made my stomach churn. It was a photo of Treece with another woman, hugging and kissing. So, Treece was what we had in common! Tears welled up instantly.

Women can be so cruel. Here I was, eight months pregnant, and Treece was intimately involved with someone else. What made it worse was that she deliberately showed me this! No wonder he hadn't bothered to call me back or check if I was okay.

I couldn't hold back my emotions. I messaged her back, demanding to know why she was in a picture with my man.

As I read her response, I felt so stupid!

"Your man? Well, if he's yours, why is he in bed with me?"

My heart raced as anger and hurt surged through me. I felt like a fool, betrayed by Treece and this woman.

I called him repeatedly, but he didn't answer, worsening my despair. Why couldn't my life be drama-free, without worries or chaos?

As time passed, I felt worse. The woman kept messaging me, bombarding me with pictures and videos of them together. It became clear that Treece had been cheating on me without remorse for some time.

I blocked the woman and sent everything to Treece's phone. Collapsing onto the bed, I stared at the ceiling until discomfort forced me to shift, struggling to catch my breath. I felt utterly defeated. The man I loved was cheating on me, indifferent to my pain. Tears streamed down my face uncontrollably.

It seemed I was destined never to be worthy of love, respect, or honor from any man. I felt like nothing more than a discarded object. As I sobbed, the phone began to ring.

I hit "Ignore" swiftly. Today, he would wait for me, just as he made me wait countless times. It was time for payback.

The rest of the day, I ignored him for well over a week. Treece didn't hear from me at all. He continued to call and I never answered. I was beyond hurt, and I didn't know what to say to him. I knew all he was going to do was lie to me.

This was just the rise of the vicious cheating cycle that Treece would be a part of. The cheating never stopped. Treece was a womanizer. He couldn't get enough of women at all.

I tried it all to keep him happy, and no matter what, there was always another woman taking a piece of him that was actually a piece of me.

Each time he cheated with someone else, my self-esteem dropped even lower, my confidence flew out the window.

I was nearing my due date, but something felt off—not physically, but emotionally, especially with Treece.

Every time I saw him or heard his voice, I felt unsettled. Despite wanting to trust and believe him, I couldn't shake the feeling of betrayal and worthlessness. It was clear he didn't love me like he said he did.

Then, confirmation came in the form of another Facebook message, this time from a woman named Tinsley in Texas. She knew everything about me, my life, and my children.

She knew so many personal things about me. Was he really out there talking about me to these women?

Yes, he was! He was making a fool out of me, and I was pregnant with his baby.

I was shattered.

"He heals the brokenhearted and binds up their wounds."Psalm 147:

Chapter 22: Strength Through Faith

Have you ever felt like a complete fool? Not because you lacked intelligence or understanding, but because people treated you like a toy, playing with your emotions right in front of your eyes?

I laughed out loud, trying to keep myself from crying. Here I was, twenty-one years old, expecting my fourth baby. To make matters worse, the father of my child didn't even respect or love me.

The stress hit me hard. Sharp pains struck my lower abdomen and radiated to my back.

Why couldn't Treece just focus on us and our relationship? I began to question everything about myself. What did those other women have that I didn't? Why couldn't I keep him happy? So many questions raced through my mind, making me feel like my brain was going to explode.

Isn't it crazy how someone else can hurt us, yet we end up blaming ourselves, thinking we're missing or lacking something?

Treece had returned to Tampa to be there for the baby's birth. Though he was physically by my side, I felt completely disconnected from him.

At that moment, I was dealing with emotional and physical pain. The sharp pains worsened, and I realized I might be going into labor.

I told Treece we needed to go to the hospital. Fortunately, all our belongings were packed weeks ago, so we left the house quickly. After dropping the kids off at my granny's, Treece drove me to St. Joseph Hospital.

We arrived just in time; Le'Tory was ready to make his grand entrance. Treece pulled up to the door, helped me into a wheelchair, and pushed me to the front desk.

The lady at the counter welcomed us warmly. She began asking for my information to get me set up for admission. Shortly after, a nurse called me to the back. Treece was parking the car and grabbing our bags. The nurse wheeled me to the back and assured me she would let Treece know where I was.

She handed me a gown and told me to ask for help if I needed anything. I changed into the gown, laughing at how it resembled an ugly, handmade moo moo dress. It wasn't flattering at all.

As soon as I got comfortable in bed, Treece walked in. The pain was getting worse, and the contractions were definitely getting closer together. The doctor came in to check how far dilated I was. You have to be about 10cm dilated before they let you start pushing.

The nurse returned and started an IV in my hand. Then, she wrapped monitors around my belly to keep track of the baby's heartbeat and my blood pressure. Hearing Le'tory's heart beating loud and clear made me so excited. I couldn't wait to see him and hold him in my arms.

Treece stayed right by my side, asking every few minutes how I felt or if I needed anything. He was the first man to be in the hospital room with me during labor. All the other times, it was just my mom or grandma. Honestly, I was relieved to have him there this time, not facing childbirth alone.

Before I knew it, I started feeling immense pressure below. I told Treece to get the nurse and let her know what was happening. He rushed to get her. The nurse returned to do another vaginal check. This time, I was fully dilated and ready to start pushing. I became so hot and nervous. Even though this was my fourth baby, I was still filled with anxiety.

The doctor came in and introduced herself, explaining she would let me know when to start pushing. The nurses were all dressed in white gowns with gloves on their hands. I began to push, and after about five pushes, my baby's head was out!

"Baby, you did it! Just one more push, and he will be all the way out!"

With one hard push, Le'Tory made his entrance! His little cry was so cute, and he was so tiny. The doctor passed him to me, laying him directly on my chest. I just began to cry, overwhelmed with emotion. I looked at his little face, fingers, and toes. Treece then leaned in close to me with giving me a kiss.

Tory was the cutest little thing. I kissed him all over and just stared at him in amazement. Treece cut the umbilical cord, and shortly after, the nurse then took to get him all cleaned up. LeTory was not having it, he was upset from being moved and was probably cold.

After he got all cleaned up, they brought him back to me, the nurses began to make sure I was ok. The next thing we had to do was get upstairs to a maternity room. After about an hour, we finally made it upstairs. They weighed LeTory and took his weight and saw how long he was. He was only 4lbs 01 oz. and about 19 inches long.

He was the smallest of all the children I had given birth to before. However, I didn't think much of it because he was perfect in my eyes. I knew the kids would all be excited to see him later.

I called my mom to let her know I gave birth and to bring the kids to me. I also called my papa, who even stopped by to see me. I was really surprised to see him. But he saw the baby and I and he even spoke to Treece briefly. I was happy to see him, honestly. The little girl in me just couldn't completely turn my heart off when it came to him. I knew one day my dad and I relationship was going to be one of the best in the entire world.

After he left, my mother brought the kids to see their new brother. They were all excited. Each of them took turns holding him and taking pictures with him.

They may have stayed for an hour. I was extremely tired and wanted to get some rest, so they left and left us at the hospital to get some sleep.

As you know, in the hospital, you can never get any rest, every time you try to close your eyes, here comes a nurse to do vitals or whatever else they were trying to do. I was just ready to go home!!

The next morning, I noticed something very strange with my baby, he wasn't hardly eating anything. I was trying to feed him a bottle yesterday and he didn't drink much. On the other hand, he began to vomit over and over. I held him on my chest and began to pat and rub his back. He squirmed a little. He seemed very much uncomfortable. He just would not stop vomiting, and I was so confused because he wasn't even drinking anything!

I wrapped him up and put him in his baby bed. I then made sure my gown was tied up properly and all my goods weren't hanging out. I then pushed him to the nurse's station. Everyone was busy on the phone. As soon as one nurse became available after hanging up from another patient, I instructed her to find out what was wrong with my baby and bring him back once they figured out what was wrong.

I walked away before awaiting an answer and went back to my room. Treece wasn't there. He checked on the kids and stopped by his mom's house. LeTory was my fourth child, so I knew something was wrong because this had never happened with any of my other kids.

After a few hours, the nurse and the doctor came back to the room with my baby and they said they were able to figure out why he was not eating and explained the vomiting. They said the baby had a lot after birth that he swallowed. They suctioned everything out and pumped his stomach for the remaining afterbirth that was there.

My baby was fast asleep and looked refreshed. I hoped everything was okay with him after this. They asked if I had any other questions before leaving my room. We were scheduled to go home in the morning, so I didn't have any questions, so I just told them no.

Treece walked in not too long after coming over to kiss me and then walking over to the baby, I then let him know everything that was going on with the baby. Treece was very overprotective when it came to him. He was ready to go back to the nursing station for more answers. However, I assured him everything was ok.

Since Treece was now there, he allowed me to rest while he looked after the baby, it just seemed I couldn't rest or get enough sleep. My back was hurting, my stomach was hurting, and my vagina just felt like it was swollen from being jumped by one hundred people!

After a few hours of rest, I woke up to Treece feeding the baby, and this time, he was indeed eating. Treece placed him over his shoulder, and Tory let out a huge burp! I giggled. "Alright, big boy!"

I was so excited that he was eating, and his little butt was over-burping as if he had eaten a state dinner. Our baby was so tiny and small, but he was so special. I loved him so much! There was nothing I wouldn't do for my little man. I kind of considered him to be my rainbow baby. I was forced to have an abortion with the baby before him, and he was my miracle. He would forever be special to me.

The next morning, we were finally released and discharged. Treece helped me gather things, and the nurses also packed the car. I held onto LeTory as they pushed us in a wheelchair downstairs. Treece buckled him inside his car seat in the backseat. I decided to sit in the back with him as we drove home. I was so happy to be out of the hospital.

We finally made it home. We were living in a 3-bedroom apartment in the Seffner area. Our neighbors were outside, and we were excited to see we were home. They ran up to us to see the baby. Treece was not having it, lol. He briefly opened the blanket covering Tory's seat and then covered it back up quickly.

As we made it to the house, I sat on the couch to just relax. The kids would be home soon. Treece began to put all the baby stuff away. Tory, of course, was asleep. Newborns had the easiest life ever; they would just sleep all day. I knew this wouldn't last long, so I was trying to prepare myself.

Treece was out on maternity leave from his job for another week before he had to go back to Texas. I was happy about that because I really needed the help.

When the kids came home, I was back in full mommy mode. Treece helped out a great deal. He made sure the kids all ate, had baths, and had everything they needed so I wouldn't have to lift a finger.

Tonight was the first night we were home alone with Tory. This was also the night of hell. Tory would not sleep at all. He was up every ten minutes. I kept trying to lay down and I just couldn't. Treece and I would go back and forth with getting up but it was to the point we just stayed up standing because this baby was screaming. No matter what we did he wouldn't stop crying. If he did he would only stop briefly.

We went on with this for the next couple of days, and we both were sleep-deprived. We were starting to argue and get angry at each other because neither of us was getting proper rest. On the fourth day of this cycle, I noticed in the middle of the night that Tory's stomach was so big. It sort of looked like he was bloated in a way. It was so tight, and when I would give it a little squeeze, his cry became even louder.

I looked at Treece and advised that it was time for us to take Tory to the hospital and figure out what was wrong. We packed up everything and took Tory to the hospital. After a long wait in the hospital lobby, we finally got called back to the back with the doctor. They examined Tory and checked everything. His vitals all came back okay. He did have a little fever, but they didn't know what was wrong with him.

I shared with them the story of what happened in the hospital, and after that, the doctor did the same treatment they gave him some gas medicine and then pumped his stomach and flushed out his lungs using air through a nose tube that would clear his airways and keep them open.

They also had him on a ventilator while we were there to deliver oxygen through a tube in the mouth.

After several hours at the hospital with the baby, Tory's stomach did indeed go down, he was as fast asleep. While the both of us were drained and beaten down. We were like walking zombies. The nurses gave us the discharge papers, which it just stated Tory had gas issues, but none of this made any sense to me. I knew something else was wrong, and these temporary fixes would not cut it.

I was going to get to the bottom of this, but for now, I just wanted to race home and get in bed. About twenty minutes later, we arrived home, and we quickly made it into the house. I left Tory in his car seat because I was so scared that if I moved him, he wouldn't stay asleep.

We immediately jumped in the bed, and I'm sure we both were snoring. Surprisingly, I was able to get three straight hours of sleep. The baby began to cry and the kids also wanted some breakfast. I grabbed Tory, and then I made his bottle. Once I got him to settle in his bassinet. I went to make cereal for the other kids. I didn't have the strength to make a full breakfast for them. I was still tired.

They all were okay with cereal, and they wanted to bother their baby brother, but I quickly gave them instructions to watch TV while mommy went and lay back down. I burped Tory, and he was fast asleep again. I tip-toed back into the room while pushing his bed back into the room with me. Treece was asleep still.

He was "super lucky,"as I thought to myself. Getting sleepy around here seemed like a privilege. I laid down in the bed and Treece grabbed me closer to him. It felt really good to be in his arms. I was happy he was around. Even though he messed up before, I'm glad he stuck around and supported me. I soon fell asleep again as well, beingcuddled in the bed right next to him.

The next couple of days were a routine of getting settled with the baby and getting accustomed to our new schedule. Treece had to leave and get on the road, and it was a Sunday. He said all of his goodbyes to us. I couldn't help but feel sad because now I was going to be all alone again, and now with four children,one of them a newborn.I guess I just had to do what I had to do.

A few months had passed, and I think I had everything under control regarding running the house with four children instead of three. Since Treece had been gone, the kids had been a big help for me, too. They would grab bottles, throw away diapers, and help me straighten up. I was just so grateful.

"Ring, Ring, Ring,"my cell phone loudly rang. It startled me, so I quickly grabbed it and said hello.

On the other end of the phone was a soft-spoken lady.

"Hello, is this the parent of Letory"?

"Yes ma'am, it is, how can I help you"? I asked.

The lady explained she was an assistant at an office called USF Pediatrics Pulmonology. She was calling with some important information regarding the baby. I sat up to make sure I was all of the way up.

She began explaining that the baby's newborn screening came back, and she went over the results. I was a little nervous because this was the first time I had ever received a call from a specialist's office.

She continues and states that upon reviewing Le'tory's newborn screening and blood work. He has been found to have a chronic disease called Cystic Fibrosis and would need to come in to have an appointment and complete a sweat test to confirm.

My emotions were all over the place. The lady over the phone was using all these big words that I didn't understand, and I didn't know what was going on. I asked her one simple question.

"Is there a cure for this disease"?

She answered, "Not at the moment, but with more testing as of right now, a child with CF is able to live up to the age of Twenty years Old"!

I literally broke down, like what in the world was going on, why did my baby have to have a disease where there was no cure? I began to beat myself up and blame myself for the reason he had this disease I had an abortion right before him. I wondered if it had something to do with that. So many crazy thoughts began to consume my mind.

I almost forgot the lady was still on the line she could hear I was crying and stated that everything was going to be o.k and that many children with CF go on to live healthy lives just like other children.

She then scheduled an appointment for us to come this week and explained that we would have a round-table meeting to discuss everything in more detail.

I hung up the phone with her and stared at the wall. What in the world had just happened? I knew something was different about Tory. Mothers just have an instinct when something isn't right. Now, I had a new perspective on life. My baby time could be limited here, and I didn't want to lose my little miracle.

Today seemed to be the beginning of the worst day of my life. I went to look at Tory in his bassinet, and he was fast asleep and cuddled under his favorite blanket. I kissed him and told him he would grow up to be strong and healthy.

After that, I called Treece to tell him the news. He was just as shocked and emotional as I was, but he reassured me that everything would be okay. I believed him and held on to my hope.

The next few days passed, and it was time for Tory's appointment at USF Pediatric Pulmonology. We arrived, and I checked him in, they called us back, and they put these devices on his arms that were supposed to collect his sweat. We had to wait about an hour for the device to complete the collection.

After it was complete, we were in the room with the nurse and collector, and they confirmed that Tory indeed did have Cystic Fibrosis. I was saddened, but it wasn't time for me to lose hope. I had to be strong for my baby. Following the collection, I was called into a room with a large brown table surrounded by black swivel chairs. So many medical professionals walked into the room.

Everyone introduced themselves and explained their roles. They explained how they were going to be moving forward with Torys medical care.

One doctor named Dr. Sneff began to explain what Cystic fibrosis was : "You may know that you have mucus in your nose, mouth, and lungs, and that it helps keep you healthy. But kids with the condition cystic fibrosis have bodies that make thick, sticky mucus. This causes problems in their lungs and their digestive tract. The condition makes it hard for them to breathe and also to get the nutrition they need from their food."

He also explained the medications that were necessary for Tory to take right before eating or drinking. They were called enzymes, which you would open up a capsule and place the pellets on applesauce and give to him. Tory's life would forever be changed from this moment and also our family. God got me out of a lot of things and I knew Healing Le'Tory from Cystic Fibrosis wouldn't be too big for God!

Although I was scared and full of fear, I stood up with confidence and boldness and let all the doctors know I appreciated them for being there for us and that I would take very good care of Tory.

We left the appointment, and I didn't really know how to pray real good, but all I could do was just sit in the driver seat and scream out "GOD HELP ME"!

Have you ever faced a challenge so daunting that it felt like your world was crumbling? The enemy has a way of deceiving us, making our struggles seem insurmountable. Yet, God never abandons us. He knows our limits and carries us through even the darkest times.

In moments like these, only God can truly provide the strength and healing we need. As Psalm 41:3 reminds us, "The Lord sustains him on his sickbed; in his illness, you restore him to full health."

As I held Le'Tory in my arms, feeling his warmth and hearing his tiny cries, I realized that despite all the heartache and betrayal, I was not alone. God was with me, guiding me, and giving me the courage to move forward. This new chapter was not just about the challenges I faced but also about the hope and faith that carried me through.

The Lord sustains him on his sickbed; in his illness you restore him to full health.- Psalm 41:3

Chapter 23: Rising Above Broken Promises

Treece and I tried to make our relationship work, but his constant cheating made it impossible. He was never satisfied with just one woman; it was like he thrived on having multiple women. I was exhausted from all these women reaching out to me, telling me they had been with him. Each of them had a piece of me.

The worst thing a man can do to a woman is to repeatedly break her spirit. I was partly to blame because I kept believing he would change, trusting his lies. The resentment I felt towards him was overwhelming.

I finally decided to move on for my own sanity, but he refused to let me go. When I confronted him yet again about another woman who had reached out to me, he blindsided me with a question I never expected:

"WILL YOU MARRY ME?"

I was so busy arguing and blaming him for disrespecting me that I didn't even realize what he was saying. In the middle of my rant, he stopped me and said, "Just leave me alone! Ash, I want to marry you!"

I held the phone in utter shock. Marry me? I thought to myself. How could this man, who was constantly cheating on me, now want to marry me? I knew Treece was no good, but somehow, the same man who broke me could also make me feel whole.

I know it sounds foolish, but I instantly became super happy and fell back in love with him all over again. This man was like a drug. I could never leave him alone. I was addicted to him and all the pain he caused me.

"Yes"! Yes! I will marry you, baby! I screamed.

Soon after that we began to start planning for the wedding.I was super excited. I hung up with him and called my grandmother to let her know. She didn't sound happy at all, however for the sake of me. She didn't project her feelings onto me.

She never liked Treece; she always said he was a womanizer and not a good man.I really felt my grandma hated me at the time. However, later on, I would find out that she had a lot of wisdom, and there was a lot of truth to everything she had been telling me.

In spite of that, I proceeded with our plans for our future wedding. I called all my friends and let them know. I even went to try on tons of wedding gowns, and I found one and bought it the same day. I left it at my Grandmother's house so Treece would never have the opportunity to see it before the wedding.

I also found the perfect venue, the wedding would be at the Intercontinental Hotel on Kennedy and Westshore Blvd in Tampa, FL. After meeting with the hotel's coordinator, I placed a huge deposit down. I was overly excited and looked forward to being the wife of Treece. I dreamed of what my life would be like. I sat there in a daydream, wondering if the marriage would make him stop cheating on me.

Who knew, it seemed to be all wishful thinking. I believe he was worth the risk. If I loved him correctly. Maybe, just maybe, one day, he would love me in that same way.

The good news is that Treece finally moved back to Tampa from Texas and was now living with me and the kids. I was so happy to have him home again. I was comfortable and at peace, and the kids even enjoyed him being around. We lived in a townhouse I had just moved into in Valrico. It was pretty big, too. Our room was a good size and had two separate walk-in closets that were huge. I didn't even have enough clothes or shoes to fill it.

Treece was the type of man who had all the latest sneakers and tons of clothing. His closet was packed with clothes! It literally looked like a men's clothing mall there. I loved how nice and neat he was, he really took pride in how he looked and always smelled so good. I thought this man was so fine, and he was all mine.

I wasn't always happy, but this temporary excitement did make me feel good.

Around this time, I had already gone wedding dress shopping and found the perfect dress.I couldn't wait to get married. It was a dream come true.

Months passed, and everything was going well until one day,Treece decided that he no longer wanted to be with me or be a family man. He decided not to say anything to me. The way I found out cut me deep to my soul. I came home from work, and I noticed a majority of his belongings were gone. I began to call him on my cell, and there was no answer. I immediately got his voicemail over and over. I sent several messages, and there was no response.

My heart dropped to the bottom of my stomach. I went upstairs, walked in his closet, and saw only a few things left. I walked to the bathroom, and his side of the counter was completely cleared. All his lotions, deodorants, colognes, etc., were gone!

Where did he go? Why did he leave? So many questions began to race through my head, and I instantly became full of anxiety. I found myself pacing the bathroom as I tried to gather my thoughts about my next move.

I grabbed my phone again and began to dial his number again. This time, it was ringing, but he didn't answer.I continued to do this for over thirty minutes and got nothing!! I raced downstairs and looked at the time on the stove. It was 4:00 p.m. That meant Treece was still at work, and I could catch him at work if I hurried.

I grabbed my keys off the kitchen counter, grabbed my purse off the couch, and ran out the door quickly. I was angry at this point because Treece repeated the same things over and over, and I was so stupid to keep allowing him to hurt me.

I turned on my radio and turned the music as loud as possible got it. It was my grandma.

"Hello,"I answered.

"Hey baby, don't forget to get Tory. I picked him up from the school, so he is here with me and I have choir rehearsal, so get your tail here fast,"demanded my grandma.

I had totally forgotten I was supposed to pick my youngest baby up from her.

"OK, Grandma. I will be there in about ten minutes."I hung up and proceeded in the direction I was going. It was a good thing her house was in the direction I was already driving. I pulled up to my granny's house. She was in the yard watering the grass while Tory was pushing a truck on the sidewalk.

I jumped out of the car, greeted my granny, and proceeded to grab Tory.He lit up when he saw me, so I covered him with kisses all over his face. He giggled so hard. I placed him in his car seat and made sure he was buckled in.

"Bye, Grandma, I love you,"I yelled as I drove away.

You could see her still watering the grass and waving her hand toward us.
I was only about fifteen minutes away from Treece's Job. I got there fairly quickly because before I knew I was pulling into the parking garage.

I could see a rush of people walking towards the garage. This was an indicator that people were getting off, so Treece should be walking out soon as well. I had made it just in time. I parked my car, got out from the backseat, and started to walk to the main entrance of the bank.

As I was walking up, one of Treece's co-workers noticed me and asked if I was looking for him. I was happy he stopped me because Treece wasn't even there. He continued to tell me that I just missed him and that he was headed to the basketball court at the Rec center up the street for a game.I thanked the guy, and my baby and I turned around to go back to the car.

So this man was just going on with his day as if he didn't see all fifty of my missed calls. My emotions were everywhere. I drove not even three minutes up the road—it was maybe a mile away. I pulled into the Rec center and got Tory out of the car. I held his hand to allow him to walk on his own with assistance.

The Rec center was a large tan building with chipped burgundy double doors and a tarnished bronze door handle barely hanging on by only one rusty nail. I pulled the door open and was greeted in the foyer by a group of men in basketball jerseys in a huddle. I said hello while quickly squeezing by them. I was on a mission to find out where Treece was.

Tory's little legs barely kept up with me because I was walking so fast. As soon as I walked in and looked toward the bleachers. I spotted Treece almost instantly. He was sitting on the third set of bleachers. He was wearing some dark gray basketball shorts and a light gray shirt with a black Nike check on it.

I noticed quickly that he wasn't alone. There was a white heavy set lady with thin blond hair sitting in between his legs on the second set of the bleachers. Treece's arms were around her neck as he leaned forward a little as they both watched another team play.

I pulled Tory along and proceeded in the direction of Treece. He turned my way and jumped up. He charged at me, picking up a Tory and pushing me out of the Gym. It all happened so fast that I didn't really get to see this woman and who he was with.

"Stop pushing me, "I screamed, as Treece forced me outside. He wasn't listening to me. Once we both got outside, he walked me and Tory to the car and told me to get in. He put the Tory in his car seat and he got in the passenger side. I got in the driver seat. I started to drive and began to ask a million questions.

"Why did you leave?, where is your stuff, and who is that lady you are with"?

He didn't answer me; he was just trying to calm me down, but at this point, I couldn't be calm. The man I was in love with was constantly playing with my heart as if it were some sort of Toy. I pulled into an abandoned parking lot, and we began to talk. He wasn't being direct with his answers, and he was lying to me.

He said that he left because he didn't feel I wanted him to be there. I was so confused. How did this man think I didn't want him there when everything was going great?

This was a major cop-out, but at the time, I didn't know. I began to cry and scream because I told him he was with that woman and I was going back to go and talk to her. I had many questions, and I just wanted to know why I wasn't good enough for this man. I think I am in a panic and being frantic, and very emotionally scared.

He then opened the door and ran from my car—like literally ran off! He ran into the woods. I saw the direction he went in, but I knew his car had to be back at the rec center and that he had to go back there. So I headed back there. I also wanted to get some understanding from this white woman sitting in the middle of his legs.

I wasn't that far away, so I pulled up to the recreation center fast. To my surprise, when I pulled up to the recreation center, the White woman had just walked to an SUV-type vehicle and closed the door. I pulled right beside her and got out. I left the truck running because Tory was still in the back seat.

When she saw me pull up next to her and get out, she locked her doors. I heard them lock as I closed my door. I went to her side of the window and asked her who she was. She was looking right at me but wouldn't answer me.

Lady, who are you, and why are you sitting between my man like that?" I demanded.

She replied, "Ask him."

"No, I'm asking you!"

This woman refused to engage with me, which only fueled my anger further. I stormed back to my truck and popped open the trunk. I was ready to grab my brother's Devil Rays baseball bat. If she wouldn't talk to me willingly, she was going to talk to me one way or another.

"I yelled at her, 'You better start talking, I promise you that!'"

Grabbing the bat from the trunk, I could see her watching me through the window as she cranked up her truck and sped off.

I slammed the trunk shut, jumped back into the driver's seat, and floored it to catch up with her. Who did this lady think she was, cozying up to my man like that, his arms around her? I yelled as I drove, my rage boiling over. I honked my horn and swerved, desperate to get her attention and make her stop.

But she wasn't stopping. Then suddenly, police sirens pierced the air. Glancing in my rearview mirror, I saw five or six cop cars flashing red and blue lights, closing in fast. The woman ahead finally pulled over in a grassy area by a red light.

I wasn't afraid of the police, nor did I care about them. Ignoring their commands, I marched towards the white lady's car. But ahead, four more cops had their guns trained on me, demanding I stop and get on the ground.

Their voices faded into the background. All I could see was red, consumed by the urge to confront the woman who had seemingly stolen what I believed could fulfill me.

Suddenly, an SUV police truck pulled up in front of me. An officer jumped out, shouting urgently at the others not to shoot.

"Don't shoot! Don't shoot!"

It was a black woman, maybe in her forties, with her hair pulled back in a bun. She stepped directly in front of me, wrapping me in a tight hug that I couldn't pull away from. As she held me close, she gently asked what was happening.

I felt a jumble of emotions—anger, embarrassment, exhaustion from feeling used and mistreated.

Tears streamed down my face as the female officer continued to hold me. She guided me to her vehicle and sat me in the passenger seat of her truck. Finally able to compose myself, I wiped my eyes.

She patiently asked me questions, and I poured out the story of Treece, the father of my son, and how he constantly cheated on me. This time, he had suddenly packed up and left without explanation. I struggled through tears to explain where I found him and what had transpired.

I had to pause several times to collect myself. The officer remained patient throughout. Then, the male officers motioned for her to join them in a huddle. They seemed to be discussing something intensely, but I couldn't make out the details over the roar of passing traffic.

Suddenly, I remembered Tory was alone in the backseat of my still-running car. I dashed back, flung open the door, and scooped him up. All eyes turned towards me as I hurried back to the police truck, settling Tory on my lap.

Then, I saw Treece emerge from a side street, running towards the white woman. They embraced, and he kissed her passionately. My heart sank, and rage boiled inside me. Surrounded by officers, I felt utterly helpless.

The black female officer approached me and asked sternly:

"Please tell me you weren't driving recklessly with this baby in the car."

I hung my head in shame, unable to answer. It was true—I had driven recklessly with my son in the car, a thought that made me feel like a failure as a mother.

She continued, pulling out her notepad:

"Here's what the other officers are discussing: You were driving recklessly to follow that woman. You had a minor child in the vehicle. Your license is suspended. And the woman claims you threatened her with a bat."

The officer leaned in, her voice filled with concern:

"All those white officers are ready to take you in. They don't even want to hear your side of the story," she confided. She went on to explain how she had listened to the woman's account and Treece's version, seeing through his manipulation. Her experience had taught her to recognize when older men exploited young women, leading to these kinds of confrontations.

"Am I going to jail?" I asked anxiously.

"No, you're not. That's why I'm glad I was here, because otherwise, you would have," she assured me.

She advised me sternly to leave Treece alone, emphasizing, "He's no good." According to her, Treece had portrayed me as unstable and denied any relationship with me.

I questioned with confusion, "He said that?"

"Yes, ma'am, he did. And he'll keep lying and manipulating the next woman, so take this as your way out," she advised firmly.

"I will, and thank you so much for helping me." Finally, my family and friend were allowed to approach. The officer engaged with my grandma and mom, and my grandma didn't hold back.

"I never liked that Joker; always a womanizer," she declared. My mom chimed in, explaining to the officer how I was supposed to be heading home instead of dealing with Treece's mess.

Brandon, my friend, crossed over to me to check in. He had a lively personality, much like mine. He wanted to confront Treece—he'd never been a fan and hated seeing how he treated me. But surrounded by officers, Treece remained protected from any immediate retaliation.

After a few minutes, the officers gave permission for us to leave, but someone would have to drive my car because I didn't have a license. My mom volunteered to drive Tory and me home.

Everyone else got in their cars, and we drove away. As we drove off, we passed by the white woman's car, and I locked eyes with Treece as he got in her car. I busted out crying.

My mom pulled me close, rubbing my arms gently. "Wipe your eyes, Ash. You deserve better. You don't have to take this from anybody. That boy ain't nobody. He's going to do her the same way, mark my words."

Her words rang true, hitting me hard. I felt shattered, foolish, and betrayed. We were supposed to get married, and now I'd have to face everyone with the painful truth: there would be no wedding after all.

I wouldn't wish this pain on anyone. It plunged me into depression, drained me of motivation, and robbed me of happiness. As a single mother of four, struggling to make ends meet without a supportive partner by my side, I blamed myself. I was the problem. I allowed this cycle to repeat, letting myself be hurt again and again.

But no more. Enough was enough. Or so I thought...

Psalm 119:50 - "This is my comfort in my affliction, that your promise gives me life."

CHAPTER 24: ENDURANCE THROUGH SUFFERING

You know, I get it. You might be thinking, "I should never go back to Tory's dad, Treece, and start talking to him again." Trust me, I wish I could say I never did. I had my moments of strength, where I wouldn't talk to him for a while. But then, like clockwork, he'd reach out with those sweet nothings, and I'd find myself back in his grip. It was like he had this hold on me that I couldn't break. He was like a drug in human form, and I kept running back for that fix.

What made it worse was that he wasn't even actively involved in Tory's life. I barely got any support from him, especially financially. Treece had other children, and Tory was just another one in his list. After he left me for that woman Jesse—yeah, I found out her name later—I had to put him on child support. It was tough, but I had to do what was best for Tory and me.

Treece always had a knack for surprises, and not the good kind. He was a compulsive liar, telling me whatever I wanted to hear. Our relationship was a rollercoaster of being together and apart over the years, but he never truly committed to me. Despite that, the chemistry between us was undeniable. He couldn't seem to live with me, yet he couldn't stay away either. It was a bizarre cycle.

Then came the bombshell: I discovered Treece had married Jesse. After their marriage, his attitude towards me turned cold and dismissive. He wouldn't answer my calls, except when they were having issues or he was bored. That's when he'd reach out with casual conversation and tell me he missed me.

With my self-esteem at an all-time low, I settled for the little attention he gave me. Each time we spoke, Treece would promise he was leaving his wife to come back to us, to give us a real family. I wanted to believe him, but deep down, I knew better. He had lied too many times before. I couldn't understand why he married her in the first place, especially after everything he said to keep me hooked.

One thing I learned was that I had come to understand Treece like the back of my hand after all those years. It was almost unsettling how well I knew him—perhaps even better than he knew himself. I realized that if I played along with his wishes, he would, in turn, fulfill my requests and give me what I wanted

The more I tried to keep peace, remain calm, and comply with Treece's wishes, the smoother our relationship seemed to go. I consciously chose to be kind and accommodating, hoping it would benefit me and my children. No more outbursts or drama—I needed stability. You might wonder why anyone would go to such lengths just for a man's kindness. The truth was, my son was sickly and needed a lot, yet child support was a measly $58.18 every other week—hardly enough to cover essentials.

Financially, I was drowning. Bills piled up—probation fees, mandated classes, rent, utilities, car payments, insurance—it was a constant struggle. Eventually, it all collapsed. I returned home one day to find an eviction notice pinned to my door. I was homeless with four children, feeling like I had failed them. Desperate, I turned to family for help, but everyone was stretched thin. Granny couldn't take us in, mom refused, and my brother's place was too crowded. It was a tough spot to be in.

I called up my best friend, Brandon, and poured out my heart to him. He was always there with practical solutions and unwavering support for me and the kids. Brandon knew just how dire our situation was and immediately suggested we stay at a hotel until we could find a more permanent solution.

With no money and feeling utterly desperate, I was willing to do whatever it took to ensure my children had a roof over their heads. I packed up all our belongings and found a local storage unit offering a special deal—$1 for the first month plus a $25 reservation fee. It was a lifeline. Our compact SUV was packed to the brim with clothes, toys, books, and everything else we needed to survive this uncertain time.

I couldn't believe this was my reality now—homeless in the same city where my family lived. It was unimaginable, especially with children in tow. I felt abandoned, left to fend for myself and my kids. I remembered what my friend had told me about the La Quinta Inn & Suites on Fowler Ave. He said a manual authorization could secure us a room for a couple of weeks, but once they discovered it was fake, we'd have to leave.

Approaching the front desk, I handed over my ID and an old debit card. The receptionist tried to run the card, and predictably, it declined. I acted surprised and flustered, pretending to be on the phone with my "bank representative," who was actually my friend playing along.

I repeated my request, pretending to navigate through the bank's automated system on the phone. The receptionist watched me closely, seemingly convinced by my performance that I was genuinely speaking with the bank.

My friend finally answers the phone, I even think he started to believe he worked for my actual bank.

My friend finally answers the phone, I even think he started to believe he worked for my actual bank.

"Thank you for Calling Chase Bank. This is Alex. How can I help you? He asked.

"Yes, Hi Alex. My name is Ashley Montgomery, and I am at a hotel trying to get a room. However, my card is declining for some reason. I checked my balance online, and the funds are there. Do you know what's going on?

"Ms. Montgomery, I'll be glad to assist you. Can I have your card number, please?"

"4808-9877-4125-4545 I replied

Ok, awesome and verify your dob and address for me.

I verified all the information.

"Okay, Ms. Montgomery, your balance is $4,987.67."We are having some technical difficulties with processing payments at this time. However, I can assist you with providing the hotel with a manual authorization number to place the funds on hold for your stay.

After I provided all the information, my friend told me to hand the phone to the receptionist, and he would take it from there.

I then pass my phone to the receptionist and tell her the bank wants to talk to her.

They talked briefly, and the next thing I knew, my friend was providing the manual authorization number. I could hear the receptionist repeating it to make sure she heard it correctly.

"Okay, so that's 900-865, Correct? That's great; it looks like it has been approved. Thank You so much."

With the keys in hand, I returned to the car with a huge smile. I texted my friend a heartfelt thank you for securing shelter for us. Deep down, I knew what we did might not have been entirely right, but I believed God understood our desperate need for a place to stay. He knew my heart.

Driving the truck to our room on the far side of the building, I only took what we absolutely needed for the night. I didn't want to risk losing everything if we were caught or had to hurriedly vacate. We were set to stay for about two weeks—a temporary haven that already felt like home.

But my happiness was short-lived. Once settled in the room, the reality hit me hard: we had shelter, but there was no money or food to feed my children.

Then I remembered seeing a sign downstairs stating that there was free breakfast from 6 a.m. to 9 a.m. every morning.I told the kids I would be right back and not to answer the door for anyone while I was gone. I ran to the elevators in the hallway and headed down to the lobby.

Once I reached downstairs, there were a few people sitting and eating breakfast and watching the news that was playing on the TV up in the corner. The newscaster was going over the weather while some sipped on their coffee.I brought a beach bag with me on my shoulder. I went to each station, throwing bagels, muffins, sandwiches, cups of fruit, yogurt, etc. in the bag. I had to get enough food to last us breakfast, lunch, and dinner.

I looked around to make sure no one saw what I was doing. Once I thought I had enough, I headed upstairs. My beach bag tote was full of enough food for tonight, hopefully.

I returned to the room upstairs, and the kids rushed to me. They all were hungry. I separated the food. Letting them know what was for breakfast, what we were going to have for lunch and also what we were going to have for dinner. I told them not to eat anything unless I told them to. I felt so low telling my kids they had to eat a certain amount of food, so we would have enough for later. They didn't deserve this and they definitely didn't understand the mess I got us into.

After all of them were fed,I decided to take a nap while they all watched TV. I laid down for what felt like maybe ten minutes at the time. When I woke up, the kids had eaten most of the food. I didn't know I was sleeping for so long.

The only thing left was a bag of chips and some apple juice.

I asked if they had eaten lunch, and my oldest Tiyrel made sure they all ate by passing out the food. He didn't want to wake me because he knew I was tired. I was scared that now we would have nothing to eat. There was nowhere I could go, and I had no money. There wasn't even anyone I could call.

So then I grabbed the bag of chips, and I said, hey, y'all have to share this Lay's potato chips ok until I can get us something else. All of them grabbed the bag so fast, fighting over it. They were yelling and screaming at one another!

Seeing that moment shattered me. I felt like the worst mother, unable to provide even the basics for my kids while we were homeless and nearly out of food. Despite having some income, it wasn't enough to make ends meet. I dashed to the bathroom, slammed the door shut, and collapsed on the floor, sobbing uncontrollably. All I could do was cry out to God. "Please, God, if you help me out of this mess, I promise to follow you faithfully. I need you now more than ever."

In that moment of desperation, I didn't hear a divine voice respond. It was a time when I knew God was real, but I was living a life torn between faith and doubt. Challenges piled up relentlessly, and it felt like the devil was intent on destroying me.

Amid my tears, it seemed like mocking laughter filled the air, and a voice whispered, "You will always fail. You're a failure. Look at your debts, your homelessness. You're worth nothing.

Tears streamed down my face, knowing every word was painfully true. I hadn't paid my car note in months, so I could practically feel the car lot closing in on me. No longer having our apartment made me feel like a fugitive, hiding from everyone.

Eventually, I emerged from the bathroom at the hotel and approached my kids. I gathered them close and said, "Listen, Mommy is going to find a way out of this. We'll have our own home again soon." Planting kisses on their foreheads, I was overwhelmed when Tiyrel wrapped his arms around me and assured me everything would be okay. They all joined in a group hug, giving me strength I desperately needed.

From that moment on, I resolved to turn things around for my children's sake. As I got up to start preparing their bath, my phone began to ring—it was my grandmother. She had cooked a meal and invited us over to eat. Relief flooded over me; we finally had a chance for a proper meal.

The children were overjoyed, and we made our way to Grandma and Grandpa's house.

Once there, the kids couldn't contain their excitement, running up to Grandma and Grandpa, showering them with hugs and kisses, and, as usual, spilling every bit of news they knew. Kids never could keep a secret if their lives depended on it.

Grandma had prepared a feast fit for a Sunday celebration: honey-glazed ham, collard greens, corn, candied yams, cornbread, and potato salad. I served up plates for all of us, and as we sat down to eat, a comforting silence fell over the table. It felt like we hadn't had a proper meal in ages. By the time we finished, our bellies were full, and our spirits lifted. Grandma had a way with food that could make any day better.

As we tidied up in the kitchen, a knock on the door interrupted us. Grandpa went to answer it, returning with news that a Spanish-speaking man was asking for me.

Confused, I approached the door, still holding a dish towel in my hand.

"Hello, sir, how can I help you?"

The Spanish guy had a notebook and a pen. He looked up and asked if I was Ashley Montgomery. I confirmed I was indeed Ashley.

"Ma'am we are here from Alberto Towing Service, who was hired from Pidi's Auto Sales. Your vehicle is being repossessed right now. You have a past due amount of $789.53."

I immediately ran outside to the car, where I met another man already connecting my car to his tow truck. I began to scream at him to get his attention.

"Hey, please let me get our stuff out of the car, please!" I begged

The Spanish guy, by this time, had met me down at the end of my grandmother's drive-through. He signaled for the bald-headed white man to put the car down so I could get my belongings. I opened the door and began getting everything out of the car. I was pulling out baskets, bags, and boxes of our things and throwing them on grandma's lawn. I was so ashamed. My grandmother's neighbors were coming outside, and they literally were watching this all go down.

My grandparents helped get the things out of the lawn and started carrying them into the house. I was so numb and broken I couldn't even cry. At this point, I just was ready to run away.

Now I was a mother of four children, Homeless and carless. My grandma saw the despaired look in my eyes, and she said, "Trouble doesn't last always, it's going to be ok"!

In my head, I replied that it was easy for anyone to say things were going to get better—just When!! I was tired; didn't God think I had enough?

I then texted my cousin Razz to pick us up and take me to the hotel room. She pulled up about fifteen minutes later, and I gathered the kids in her car. She then dropped us off.

We stayed at the hotel for almost two weeks. A day before checkout, the room phone rang, and I went into a complete panic. Why was the phone ringing? No one even knew where we were except my friend and my cousin. They would call my cell phone.I remember Brandon telling me that if they called, they were probably going to ask you to come down with another form of payment.

I rushed to get the kids and told them to get their shoes. We ran to the elevators and down the stairs. Instead of going near the lobby, we exited out a side door of the hotel building.I googled another La Quinta Inn near us. I wanted to get another couple of weeks so I could have time to find an apartment. The closest was the Brandon area. So we caught the city bus to Brandon and repeated the same exact process, and it worked!

At this hotel, I called my papa (remember my biological dad who was never around) to let him know where we were and what was going on. He came over to see us. I told him I didn't have much money or food for them, and I was trying to figure everything out. He passed me $40 and chatted with us for a little, but that was it. I mean, no one extended their home to us. Nobody. I still had hope that things would be better soon.

A while ago, a friend suggested I apply for social security for my son, who was diagnosed with Cystic Fibrosis. I didn't know the process so she helped me do everything. I applied but never heard anything from them. She said that they would provide monthly funds for him and that would help me out a great deal!

My phone rang from 1(800) numbers I didn't recognize. I answered it, and it was the Social Security office. The young lady on the other line said she sent a letter of approval, but it was returned to her, and she wanted to make sure the address on file was correct. I updated the address using my grandmother's address and advised we had just moved. I dared not to tell her we were homeless, living in a hotel.

When she explained that his benefit was approved, I lit up! But I really became full of joy when she said the amount due to retroactive pay. I was looking to get almost $3000 in the mail!! I was so happy, and all I could do was say thank you, Jesus! Even when family and friends turned their backs on me, I was still making it because God was looking out for me!

We lived in a hotel for about a month. I received the check from my grandmother, and at that time, I was able to find an affordable three-bedroom apartment.I was able to get all of our things out of storage and was slowly piecing my life back together.

It was around this time, the month of August, and School was getting ready to start for the kids. Due to me just moving and paying all these fees, I was not able or prepared to buy my kid's school clothes. So I was forced to ask Treece to help me get them ready for school. Surprisingly, he agreed with no rebuttal at all.

I was happy he agreed to assist me with their stuff. I have to admit though, I was always bothered he had a whole entire family outside of my own. I knew he had a wife, and he had to go home at night to be with her. However, I was only around to get what I needed for my kids, all that other stuff didn't matter anymore. I thought he would understand this and just take care of what he needed to to keep me calm but he didn't care. Treece thought he could do whatever, like he was untouchable.

Treece was very good with dressing the kids. All I had to do was provide the sizes. He then got everything and came over with bags of clothes, school supplies, and backpacks. He did this for all the kids, too! Not just for Tory, I was so appreciative of the help. He seemed to be in a rush, he said hello and hugged all the kids, hugged me, and said he would call me later. I didn't cause a fuss and thanked him as he was on his way.

A month passed, and we were in September. My Grandmother was diabetic and had been admitted into the hospital for having a stroke and her sugar levels being so high. She was doing a little better, so they admitted her into a medical rehab center called "John Knox Village." The stroke she had, made her mouth turn to the left, and was pretty much stuck there. She couldn't talk all that clearly. When she spoke, she slurred.

My brother and I visited her every week, a couple of times a week. I was just so ready for her to be released. The doctors were going to discharge her soon. I was just ready to take care of her. I know she was, too, because she told me how when she got out she was going to open up her daycare and keep the kids for me.She would always ask how they were at the new daycare and schools. One thing about my granny: sick or not, baby she was going to speak her mind!

My grandmother looked so different, so unlike herself—quiet, defeated. I missed her loud laughter, her blunt humor. Seeing her in the hospital and rehab broke my heart. I prayed endlessly for her to come back home, but maybe it just wasn't meant to be yet.

The next day, as I drove the kids to school, my phone rang. I was approaching a stoplight near my house when my mom's crying voice filled the car.

"Mom, what's wrong?" I asked, my heart racing with worry.

Through tears, she struggled to speak clearly. "She's gone," she finally managed to say.

Romans 5:3-5 flooded my thoughts. In the midst of our suffering, I found solace in knowing that through it all, God's love sustained us, molding our endurance into character and our character into hope.

Romans 5:3-5 Not only that, but we rejoice in our sufferings, knowing that suffering produces endurance, and endurance produces character, and character produces hope, and hope does not put us to shame, because God's love has been poured into our hearts through the Holy Spirit who has been given to us.

Chapter 25: The End of the Road

My mother finally managed to convey clearly what she was trying to say.

"Ash,your grandma has passed away," she exclaimed.

"She's dead?!" I blurted out, stunned. "SHE'S DEAD???????!"

It took a moment for the realization to sink in, and then I remembered the kids were in the car, watching me closely. Tiyrel's face showed worry and fear, and I glanced at the other kids in the back seat. There was only one person this news could possibly be about.

Quickly, I changed my tone and forced a laugh. "Oh, girl, you scared me! I thought you were joking," I said, trying to lighten the mood.

The kids returned to their chatter, unaware of the tension a moment ago.

But my mother persisted urgently, "Ash, this is serious! Get to the hospital ASAP!"

Realizing the gravity of the situation, I replied, "Okay, as soon as I drop off the kids, I'll be there."

I was trembling uncontrollably, my nerves on edge from the devastating news. It was a struggle to keep the car steady on the road, my heart weighed down like it had shattered into a million pieces. Each breath felt like a struggle, my chest tightening with anxiety.

But I had to hold it together, for my children's sake. They couldn't handle this right now.

"You've got this, Ash," I whispered to myself, though I didn't believe it.

Arriving at the kids' school, I signed them in mechanically, trying to appear composed. Once they were settled, I hurried back to my car. Racing to my brother's apartment, just a short drive away, I felt my hands tremble on the wheel. I didn't know how I was going to break him this news.

Pulling into the nearest parking spot, I left the car running and hastily threw it into park before leaping out. I sprinted up the stairs to my brother's second-floor apartment, my heart pounding with urgency. I pounded on his door like I was trying to break it down, the sound echoing through the hallway.

"Boom, Boom, Boom!" I shouted his name, my voice desperate.

It felt like forever before he finally opened the door. His face was etched with concern, eyes wide with alarm.

"What's wrong?" he exclaimed, his voice strained with worry.

I collapsed to my knees, tears streaming down my face in torrents. I was sobbing uncontrollably, and my brother kept asking me urgently what was wrong.

Finally, I managed to choke out the words through my tears, looking up at him with blurred vision, "Grandma died! She's gone, Shard, she's gone!"

My brother recoiled in shock, his face contorting with disbelief. "What? No, no!" he shouted, tears welling up in his eyes.

"She is, Shard. We need to get to the hospital," I said, my voice trembling with grief.

He hurried inside to prepare, wiping his tears away hastily. I waited on the porch, staring up at the sky, feeling a profound sense of loss and searching for answers. Why did this happen now? Why take away the one person who loved me unconditionally?

A few minutes later, my brother emerged, ready to drive. I handed him the keys, and we pulled out of the complex. As we drove silently towards the hospital, tears still streaming down my face, my brother's expression was grim. We rode in solemn silence, the weight of our loss heavy between us.

Suddenly, my brother released the steering wheel and collapsed, burying his head in his hands as he sobbed uncontrollably. Fear gripped me, and I shouted in panic, "Pull over! You can't drive; I have to!"

He snapped out of his despair, lifting his head abruptly, and veered the car to the side of the road.

I sprang into the driver's seat while Reishard moved to the passenger side. I knew I had to be strong for both of us now. Seeing him like this, I realized we were both drowning in grief, unsure how to stay afloat. I held his hand, rubbing his back gently, trying to reassure him that everything would somehow be okay.

But deep down, I didn't know how we would navigate life without our beloved grandma. She was our "Big Mama," like the matriarch in the Soul Food movie, holding our family together. She commanded respect and love from everyone. She was my guardian angel, and now I felt utterly alone.

Driving to University Community Hospital on Bruce B. Downs and Fletcher Ave felt like an eternity. When we arrived, my mom, grandaddy, and grandma's friend, Mrs. Tolbert, were waiting in the lobby. We hugged my grandaddy and mom tightly, then embraced Mrs. Tolbert, who had been by my grandma's side for years. Tears stained everyone's cheeks; grief hung heavy in the air.

My mom found a nurse who escorted my brother and me to see Grandma. The nurse swiped her badge, and the double doors opened into a quiet medical area. Anxiety gripped me as we approached the closed door; I wasn't prepared for what awaited us inside.

The nurse gently pushed open the door, revealing a dimly lit room where Grandma lay under a white blanket on the bed. I pulled the blanket back from her face, and she looked so serene, as if she were peacefully sleeping. Her slight lip turn from a previous stroke was more pronounced now. Her hair, braided into six large plaits by my mom a few days ago, framed her face.

My brother moved to her right side, kissed her, and broke into a loud cry. I leaned in, kissed Grandma's hand, and held it in mine. Her hand wasn't warm, nor was it cold—it was just there, lifeless. She had passed some time ago, and guilt washed over me. I blamed myself for not being there for her when she needed me most.

A Black doctor entered the room, introducing himself with condolences for my brother and me. He explained that Grandma had fought hard to stay with us but eventually couldn't hold on any longer.

The doctor reassured us that Grandma hadn't experienced any pain during her passing, which brought some comfort to my heart. However, I couldn't shake the thought of what the roommate had mentioned about Grandma trying to communicate something to the nurses. It pained me to wonder what she might have been trying to say.

According to the roommate, Grandma had been hot and sweating, struggling to make herself understood due to the effects of her stroke. It must have been frustrating for her, wanting to convey something important but unable to do so clearly.

I expressed my gratitude to the doctor for his care and for sharing these details with us. Leaning over Grandma, I kissed her forehead and thanked her for everything she had done for me and my children, telling her how much I loved her. I had always expressed my love to her, but now I wished she could hear me one last time. The finality of her passing hit me hard; it was a stark reminder of how quickly life can change.

Reflecting on the moment, I realized a crucial lesson: cherish and appreciate loved ones while they are with you, because you never know when they may be gone. I wished desperately that this could all be a bad dream. My brother and I remained by Grandma's side a little longer, silently keeping vigil, before eventually returning to the lobby to wait for the funeral home to arrive and take her body away.

I sat down and sent a message to Treece, informing him of my grandmother's passing. To my surprise, he rushed to the hospital with remarkable speed. By the time he arrived, he was on the phone, a picture of professionalism in his crisply ironed khaki pants, royal polo shirt, and polished brown shoes.

As he approached me, he wrapped me in a comforting embrace. His presence alone brought me solace, and I allowed myself to lean into his support. Each time he was near, I felt a wave of relief wash over me; his strength was a balm to my grief. He stayed by my side for a while before needing to return to work, promising to come back later once he was off duty. I thanked him sincerely for being there when I needed him most.

Shortly after Treece left, I received a call from Javari, who lived nearby. I shared the heartbreaking news with him, and without hesitation, he said he was on his way. Before I could mention that Treece had already arrived, Javari was already en route to the hospital.

When Javari arrived, I walked up to him, and he enveloped me in a warm hug. He asked about the kids and if everyone was okay. Standing at 6'1", Javari always seemed to tower over me, and his presence brought a comforting familiarity. His visit meant a lot to me, especially in this difficult moment. He didn't stay long, likely noticing Treece sitting by the entrance doors of the hospital, and quickly said his farewells.

After they both left, it was time for me to pick up the kids from school and break the heartbreaking news. I dreaded being the one to tell them. Why did this have to be real? Why couldn't it all just be a bad dream?

Once everyone was in the car, I told them that when we arrived at their great-grandma's house, I had something important to tell them. We pulled into the driveway, which was crowded with cars. I instructed the kids to meet me in the back room so we could talk privately. They followed me into my uncle Jr.'s room and sat on the bed, waiting for the news.

I started by saying "today I received terrible news that is going to change our lives forever. Today your great grandma has passed away". They all looked crazy and were shocked and then asked what did pass away mean? I explained it meant that someone has now died and went to heaven. They began to cry and hug one another. I joined their group hug and didn't let go until they told me to. After we all were able to have our moment and began to process the news together we went outside where everyone was.

People were stopping by to see us in droves. So many faces—some familiar, many I didn't even know. But my granny, she knew everyone. She was a well-known musician, leading a women's group called the O'halo's, and married to my grandaddy, a member of the Southern Tones gospel group.

Despite all the commotion, none of it felt real. The days dragged on, filled with preparations and visitors, until it was finally time for her funeral a couple of weeks later. I had to speak that day. As we arrived at the church, they called me up to share my memories of her. I felt a wave of nerves and fought to hold back my tears.

I told everyone how much I loved my granny and what she meant to me and my kids. Standing there, I realized how much I was like her. I was the miniature version of Barbara Williams—bold, outgoing, and always speaking my mind. She was a force to be reckoned with, and no one ever questioned where they stood with her. At that moment, I felt proud to carry a piece of her spirit within me.

I giggled as I said that. After the service, we headed to the burial site. I couldn't bear to watch them lower my granny into the ground, so I walked away and stood by the gate, my heart breaking. This was literally the worst day of my life, and all I wanted to do was run away. Once she was buried and

119

everyone had said their final goodbyes, I took the kids and headed back to my granny's house. That's when reality hit me like a freight train.

Walking into the den, I saw my grandaddy sitting there, looking lost. I began to cry and break down uncontrollably. It came out of nowhere. I had been holding it together for everyone else, being strong when I needed to be. But now, I couldn't be strong anymore. My grandma had died, and the harsh reality was that she was never coming back.

Even when someone close to us passes away, life goes on. My granny would have wanted me to be strong and to be the best person I could be for my kids. From that day forward, I promised myself that I would do everything I could to become the best mother and person possible. I wanted to make her proud.

Later that night, Treece came by as promised. He brought dinner for the kids and helped me get them all settled for bed. After such a long, exhausting day, I was mentally, emotionally, and physically drained. I took a hot shower and then joined him in bed. He gave me a soothing body massage that almost knocked me into a coma, and I felt incredibly relaxed.

We lay in bed watching a movie, just enjoying each other's company. He stayed for hours without any rush to leave. I snuggled into his arms and soon found myself drifting off to sleep. Hours later, I woke up to Treece kissing my neck and giving me a passionate kiss. He whispered that he was coming home again. I let him talk, knowing full well that nothing could keep this man by my side permanently.

One thing led to another, and soon we were making love. Being with Treece always felt right. He was a charmer and a pleaser, doing anything to ensure I was happy. He was soft and sensual with me, making me feel like the only girl in the world. Every time we were together, it felt like our first time. I would forever be in love with this man.

I didn't want to seem too clingy, so I told Treece he should head home before it got too late. He sat up and asked, "Are you sure? I was going to stay with you."

"Yes, I'm sure. I'll see you tomorrow," I replied.

He got up and began to get dressed. Before leaving, he gave me a big hug, holding me close as he kissed my forehead

It was so strange, what was happening between Treece and me. Something just didn't feel entirely right. However, a part of me didn't care because I justified my actions by reminding myself that I was his fiancée first. But it cut me deep knowing that Jesse had made it to "wife" status before me.

I knew this wouldn't last long, and I was painfully aware of how unhealthy this connection and situationship was. I needed a way out, a way to move on with my life that didn't involve settling like this. Here I was, involved with an already taken man, acting as if I were the prize. But in reality, I was just a placeholder, having a good time.

God knew the plans He had for me, so He removed Treece from my life involuntarily because He knew I wouldn't leave him on my own. I ended up getting into some domestic trouble with him and his wife, which led to me being on probation for two years. I lost my job at the time, which then forced me to take on two low-paying jobs just to try and make ends meet.

I worked at Boston Market and Rainbow clothing stores for two years. I was required to take anger management classes and therapy and also pay all these probation fees.I was banned from reaching out to Treece or his wife, since they were considered victims. The judge ordered "NO CONTACT" He warned that if I had any type of contact then I would violate my probation and then I would be sent to Jail.

I wasn't going back to Jail for nobody.So this was the end of the road for me and Treece finally and for good!

2 Timothy 4:2- I have fought the good fight, I have finished the race, I have kept the faith.

CHAPTER 26: UNPLANNED PATHS

Now I was trying to rebuild my life and fit all the puzzle pieces back together again. It was so hard getting over Treece and not speaking to him. We used to talk every single day a couple times a day and we would never leave eachother alone. However this time was different. I didn't want to be locked up and away from my children, so I had to release him.

I remember deleting our text messages threads, all of our pictures. I threw all the gifts he bought me. Everything that reminded me of Treece I got rid of. If I was going to start a new life, I had to eliminate the old. I think that was one of the toughest things that I ever had to do, was say goodbye to someone I was deeply in love with.

However my kids mattered more to me than him, and honestly he definitely wasn't going to come before them. The disconnection was very hard in the beginning. I would find myself picking up my phone to dial him and immediately changing my mind. He was on my mind often. However as the days passed, weeks passed and then a month. I was completely over Treece. I wasn't even thinking about him once I reached the two-month mark.

I was happy where I was in life.I moved into a new apartment, closer to a new job that I was supposed to start working . My best friend Brandon and I were scheduled to start at the same company.

Just when I thought my life was good, and everything was going well. I noticed I missed my period.And im like I haven't been stressed or anything. I wasn't even having sex,so the possibility of being PREG-.......

In the middle of my thought of possibly being pregnant, I remembered the night me and treece had sex. The night my grandmother died! Omg, was I pregnant again!!! My anxiety shot through the roof. I became nervous and full of fear. I didn't need another baby at all.

I decided to do a test when I got home to confirm. It was just my luck that I was indeed pregnant again. I told Treece that he wasn't upset but wasn't full of joy either. You know he was married, so how would he explain this to his wife?
That was none of my business. I just needed to get prepared for now for baby #5.

Since I wasn't new to this, it wasn't much that I didn't know how to do already. I already had four kids, and caring for them came easy for me because I was doing it all alone for so long.I wished I could have raised my kids in a family setting.Sometimes life just doesn't go as planned unfortunately. I wasn't the type of woman to complain, I just put my big girl panties on and kept it moving.

So months passed and the recruiter from the company I was supposed to start in, advised that she had to change my class start date to a later date. This really worried me because that means it would be around the time I was supposed to have my son.

Yes I had found out I was having yet another boy! I decided to name him Trenton.Initially I was naming him after Treece like I did with Tory. I was going to name him Le'Teri but last minute I changed his entire name.This is because Treece just wasn't involved of course.

At the time of me giving birth to Trenton, he didn't even answer the phone. I sent texts, emails and called several times back to back. He never even tried to call me back. I felt so alone. However my friend named Willine was in the delivery room with me to support me.

I don't know why I expected anything different from Treece, but look, my feelings weren't hurt this time. I was so used to this behavior. I was over it. I was focused on becoming a better person and mother and getting my life together. I gave birth to Trenton on June 10, 2014. I didn't have any help at home. I was a single mother with now five children to care for. I missed my granny at this moment. I would have all the support in the world. She would take care of me, she would allow me to rest. She also would go off on me if I was doing too much!

I could hear her right now scolding me about having a "Set-back"! I found myself chucking to myself. I made sure to take it easy. Then my phone began to ring. It was the recruiter again. She called to inform me that training will start this upcoming Monday morning at 9am est.

I jumped in a panic! My baby was only about two days old and now I was required to start work. I couldn't make a decision not to go, because I was the only person bringing income in and I was already all alone with no help.I couldn't even take a normal maternity leave. So I was forced to start work just a few days after having a newborn. My baby couldn't start daycare until he was at least 6-weeks old. So my brother helped me watch him during the day since he was off at that time.I loved how my brother helped me out because he knew I had no other way to provide for my kids.

Around that time my best friend Brandon introduced me to a set of identical twin girls.They were beautiful to and fun to be around. The first one I met was named Antonetta which we just call netta. She was single and she didn't have any children and she lived alone at the time. The second twin was Antoniqua but we call him Niqua. She was pregnant at the time and had a son who was maybe around two or three years old at the time.

Netta was the twin that worked with me and Brandon and she was so helpful. Since I had just had a newborn. I tried to limit the amount of walking that I needed to do. I would only get up to go to the restroom and when it was time for lunch.When I did have to get up I walked extremely slow. Netta would walk with me and hold onto my arm making sure that I was ok. I really appreciated her for help. She was an angel sent from heaven.

We all hit it off great and became very close over the next few months.We hung out all the time, I met the rest of the twin sisters and we became real life sisters too!

On September 11, 2014 niqua gave birth to my niece Niq-Niq. I couldn't wait to see them and definitely couldn't wait to see the baby to spoil her.After work one evening I confirmed with Netta that I would be stopping by to come and see all of them at the hospital.I couldn't wait to get there.I picked up my son who was now around 2 months old, from my brother house and then headed to the hospital.

As I walked in the women's center lobby, I checked in with the front desk. As I was finishing up I could see Netta waving at me to let me know where she was. I quickly ran over to her and we began briefly talking.In the middle of our conversation. A black guy wearing a Jamaican hat ran right into us to get by.

"I was looking so confused and thought to myself about this random man running right between us!

"How Rude"I blurted out.

Then netta out of nowhere says "Girl that's just my brother. I had known Netta for about four months and I didnt even know they had a brother. They never mentioned it to me at all. He had a different mom and didn't live in the same household with them while growing up.I just giggled because I was more relieved that he was family vs it being someone we just didn't know.

Netta and I began to go down the hall to reach the elevators.We both got on the elevator and headed to the sixth floor. This was the maternity ward floor. We finally reached the floor that Miqua was on and walked into the room. I was greeted by Niqua sitting up in the bed while talking to two guys.

The man she was talking to was sitting against the wall on the benches. One of the guys was the one that ran into us. Remember this was the guy who was wearing the Jamaican hat. After being introduced to the other young man, it was Niq-Niq's father. We called him AJ. While in the room we had a great conversation. I mean we were just having a good time.

I know the nurses must have been wondering what in the world was going on in the room with all the loud laughing that was going on. We were all just having a good time.I really needed this moment of laughter and fellowship. Being a single mother nowadays is a lot. I was now a mother of five children. That was a very hard task on some days.

As we all continued to laugh and talk and joke around, Time was passing, and I knew I had to start getting back to get my other kids from my mom and head home. I began to tell everyone goodbye, as I packed my son up and placed him back in his carseat. Remember the rude guy that ran into me and netta in the lobby area.

Yes the twins brother, well his name was Royce. He offered to help me and walk me down to the car. I agreed but went into the bathroom before I was heading out.

At the time what I didn't know was that he was asking the twins for my phone number and they both declined to give it to him. They both knew I just left a very difficult situation with Treece and they definitely didn't want me hurt again.

I came out of the bathroom and he took matters into his own hands and asked if he could have my number to chat sometimes. I looked at him crazy at first. Royce wasn't the type of man I would normally talk to. He was a little shorter, maybe around 5 '9 and he was a little bigger than my ex's, however his personality was amazing. So I asked "Why should I give you my number"while laughing.

He was really getting ready to explain but then began to take his jamaica hat off, He must have become hot. When he removed his hat completely, these long beautiful dreads fell down his back!! Whhhewww I had a thing for a man with dreads. I looked and said OOOOKKKKAAY! And quickly gave him my number.

Then I said bye to the twins and AJ and we both headed down stairs to the lobby. He carried my son Trent in his carseat. As I made it to my truck outside, he helped me buckle him in and said he would talk to me later. I gave him a hug and got into my truck and drove off.

The weekend seemed to have flown by because it was already back to business on Monday morning. Weeks had passed and Trenton was now attending daycare with the other kids at a daycare right up the street from the school.

I dropped them off and then began to head to work. I always met netta and Brandon in the morning. We would get breakfast before going into our training class. We were always together. If one of us was late or missing, people in our class would ask one of us where the other one was!

On my lunch break, my phone started ringing. I didn't recognize the number. It was a 352 area code. I decided to answer it.

"Hello"? I answered.

"Hey what's up Ash"? The other voice said. Well it was a given that this person knew me but it was clear. I had no idea who it was.

"Hey, Who is this"? I asked

"This is Royce, I'm the dude you met at the hospital."

"OOOHH Yeah, heyyy! How are you"?

"I'm good, just waking up, about to get ready for the day, he said

"Oh wow it's almost 1pm and you're just getting up? I asked.

He explained how he works nights as a janitor cleaning commercial buildings, however he did have a mid day building that he had to complete that was located in lakeland.

I thought that was good that he was working, there were a lot of bums doing nothing with their lives. We chatted for a few minutes and mentioned he wanted to see me soon. He lived in Clearwater. That was across the bridge from me, so I thought it was really far at first.

So we made plans to connect that weekend. We both kept our word. Royce asked where I wanted to eat, and stated to let him know and he would meet me there. I chose the Waffle House. He paused for a moment and wanted to verify that I really meant "THE WAFFLE HOUSE"... I confirmed yes.

There was one that was right off the interstate in westshore across the street from the westshore mall in Tampa. I arrived and went to be seated. Royce pulled up shortly after and came to sit with me. I ordered my normal. A Waffle kind of crispy and a large order of bacon and a sprite. I asked him if he wanted to order. He said he wasn't hungry. So we sat and chatted as I ate.

After I was done eating, we werent ready to go home just yet so we just talked outside for a while for the rest of the night.This was the beginning of us begging together every day from there. We would take turns commuting to each other's places to hang out. I lived right by the cross town and it took me directly to his house in about twenty minutes and the same for him.

I enjoyed our time together, I always had a good time with Royce. The biggest thing was I was able to be myself. He accepted my goofiness. He also already knew I had five children and still wanted to talk to me. That was a huge and major insecurity of mine. Would I ever be able to be a woman someone wanted to talk to with five children that wasn't biologically his?

I just was enjoying the times and the moments we were spending with one another. By this time we had been talking for a few months. All of it went by so fast. We were with each other every day just about.I found myself falling for Royce and I didnt even expect this. He was so different from the other men I had ever dated. He was sort of a bad boy. I think his edginess is what drew me in. Royce would hang out with his friends however from Thursday night through Saturday nights. I would see him sunday-Wednesdays for the most part. He was like a club hopper with his friends.

So back to my point,at this particular time in our relationship more kids weren't even a thought. I was on birth control pills and took them faithfully because if you looked at me I was pregnant! We were just enjoying eachothers company really. I don't think either was thinking of anything more of it.

However, I wasn't very good at taking my birth control pills sometimes. This particular week I forgot to take them twice. So when I remembered day three, I assumed it would be a good idea to take three birth control pills all at once to catch myself up. EPIC FAIL!!!

Oh boy was this a terrible idea. I became so sick! I was throwing up, I had a massive migraine and I felt dizzy. I stayed in bed all day and didn't want to do anything. In fact I couldn't do anything. My kids had to help look after Trent. He was a baby too, so I had to watch them . It was a complete mess.

I called my cousin Razz to tell her I wasn't feeling good, because we had plans to get lunch. When I told her what was happening she told me to take a pregnancy test. I was so confused. I'm like why? I'm on birth control. There is no need for me to take a pregnancy test. She was not convinced and told me she would check on me a little later.

I laid down and now that's all I was thinking about "Could I be pregnant"? Yes by this time me and Royce were sexually active however I was on birth control and I thought I wasn't worried. Later on that day, I decided to get out of bed and at least confirm I wasn't pregnant. The thought of this was driving me crazy! I literally had just had a baby.

So I come back from Walgreens and I run to the restroom and sit on the toilet as I hold this stick while I tinkle on the tip of it. I swear the anxiety you get while waiting for the results of a pregnancy test is the worst! It's like the longest wait time in America. It seemed like a lifetime.

A few minutes passed and now I'm shaking in my boots to look at this stick. I started pacing the bathroom floor back and floor. Then I finally pause and try to peek at the stick. This was the craziest situation ever. I've been here before. I shouldn't have been acting like this. So I finally fully look at the stick and right before my eyes this stick has two pink lines!

NOOOOOOOOOOOOOOOOOOO! I scream to myself! I can't be! I began to cry. I already had enough on my plate right now , this was going to be a natural disaster. I was trying to calm down but I became so scared. I couldn't help but to think what in the world was Royce going to do? What was he going to say?

Royce already had two kids of his own. A boy and a girl from two different women. At this time I haven't met them as of yet. All I knew is that they both lived in Ocala and he only saw them occasionally when his mother and sister would bring them down. He also jumped on the road a lot to go and see them.

I decided to go and see him the next day. Everytime we were together we would always go somewhere and eat. So I planned to have lunch. We went to what was our favorite spot on his side of town. It was a pizza hut joint at the corner. We would dine in and eat and then go back to the house and enjoy movies together.

So when I met up with him, I tried to act as normal as possible. I was a nervous wreck. Today was the day I was going to let Royce know he was going to be a dad to a new little one. When we got back to his house we both were sitting on the couch and I mentioned there was something I had to tell him.

He stopped what he was doing and said "Talk".....
I froze for a minute. Then I just spat it out. If I took too long to say something then I was never going to tell him.

I just found out that I am pregnant the other day and wanted to tell you. So what are we going to do?

He was so calm and really didn't show he was mad, upset or scared or anything. He just said okay we were going to be good. My heart was at rest, however I was still a little confused that he didn't have much emotion. I remember this same response when I told Javari I was pregnant back in the day and how he flipped on me as soon as I drove off.

I was praying this wasn't a repeat. Although I didn't need anymore kids, I always felt like God allowed things to happen for a reason. Why would God allow me to get pregnant if he didnt think I could handle it? It was going to be really hard, but at least this time, I had someone by my side to stick around and really help me.

I had held my pregnancy a secret from my family for a while. I don't know why I was grown and still scared to tell them that I was having another baby. I really didn't feel like hea alringl the negative stuff, and wasn't sure of how they would accept the news. So everyone would find out later on. For now this was just our little secret.

I headed home because it was now time to get the kids. Royce had good timing because as soon as I got home I received a text from him. It basically was saying he wasn't ready for another baby and we needed to weigh our options. What the heck did that mean? What other options did we have besides that we were now parents to a baby coming soon???

Yup you guessed it. Royce wanted me to get an abortion. He even offered to take me and pay for it. I called my friend Sheneika at the time and told her what was going on, and asked her what should I do? I couldn't call anyone else because I didn't want all these people in my business. She was a great support system. She didn't believe in abortions, but she told me that whatever decision that I made she would support. So here I was contemplating whether I should get an abortion or not.

I was so tired of being in this situation.Ugh it seemed like I never was going to learn. I became depressed and sad. Royce and I began to argue and then it went a little minute that I didn't even speak to him. I had given him a key to my house but he never ever used it. I was always at home with the kids and never went anywhere, so if he wanted to find me he could.

Out of nowhere I'm sitting on the couch in the living room and he unlocks the door and walks through the door. When I looked up at him towards the kitchen. I was excited to see him, but I didn't want to show it so I just sat there. I was waiting until he walked over to me.

Royce wasn't the affectionate type so you wouldn't like him being all lovey dovey with you. He walked over and said "What's up". I replied well nothing much. What's up?

He tells me to get ready so we can go grab some food. I'm glad he did because I was starving! I got my shoes and headed out the door with him to Steak N' shake that's right up the street.

Isaiah 55:8-9 For my thoughts are not your thoughts, neither are your ways my ways,"declares the Lord. 9 "As the heavens are higher than the earth, so are my ways higher than your ways and my thoughts than your thoughts.

Chapter 27: Family, Faith and Challenges

After that, Royce and I grabbed food. We then headed back to my apartment and sat on the couch, having a long talk. Royce wasn't a guy who expressed his feelings, but tonight, it was really different.

I fell for Royce very fast. That was my downfall; I became emotionally connected to the people I dated very fast, especially if we became sexually active. You know, as women anyway, we are just naturally emotional people who think and love with our hearts vs. our minds at times.

Months before tonight I told Royce that I loved him. It was really early, too. I think it was just a couple of weeks of us talking. To be honest, I knew I had strong feelings. It felt like Love. I really cared for him and thought about him constantly when we were not around each other. So he responded by saying I didn't love him and not to say that right now because it's too early for all that!"

Boy, my feelings hurt, and I was crushed. But maybe he was right. Did I really love him, or was this lust? I stood on, that I loved him. I said all of that to say this: Royce professed his love for me about 3 months later.. He said, "I can be a man and say I do love you" and I knew that took a lot for him to say. I grabbed him by his neck and gave him a big hug. I still felt the same.

Something about him just really drew me to him. He was so different from any other man I had ever dated. He was sorta a bad boy, like a street dude. A little rough around the edges. He was spontaneous, and he was fun! Like I never could get tired of being around him. And everyone who knows me knows I get aggravated by people very fast. On the flip side, although he was a little hood, He was a hard worker! I never seen someone top his work ethic. He worked with his dad doing commercial cleaning and had several buildings to do, and he would bust them doing so fast at night.

Around this time, we decided to be together and work on our relationship. I decided to keep our son. Although he wasn't planned, we had to make the best of it. We were going to name him Trevian. I remember Royce sending a picture of my pregnant stomach to his mother, Tasha, and his little sister, Shaniya. They were super excited to meet me, and I was too.

I was sort of a secret to everyone with Royce. He was very private when it came to his personal life. I had held a secret about my being pregnant for as long as I could. I was around eight months, and now everyone knew I was pregnant again with my sixth child. I was so happy the cat was out of the bag. I was sick of keeping it to myself.

In August, I gave birth to our Son Trevian. He was such a beautiful chocolate baby boy, too. I was so happy to hold him in my arms. Despite all the junk Royce talked about before our son was born, you saw how he melted when he was holding him as well.

I must admit our relationship was sped up, and it kind of happened so fast I felt like I didn't have any control over it. We soon moved together, and one thing about me was that I was a woman who made sure men were in their children's lives. So Royce had two other children outside of me from two different women.

He grew up in a small country city called Ocala, so the kids and their moms lived there. His oldest was his son, Roy Roy, and his daughter, Aaliyah. When I met them, Roy Roy was five, and Aaliyah was three years old. It was a joy to have all of the kids around each other. They all got along most of the time, and when I tell you, our house was never a dull moment.

Royce & I were raising them the best way we knew how. We didn't have anyone to look up to for guidance. No one in either of our families was married with the amount of children that we had. Also, even if they were married, we didn't know how to decipher them having a healthy, stable marriage. It was a lot of cover-ups, secrets, lies, and deception. Marriage didn't seem like something that people took seriously. They would only count the number of years they were together as success but were really living miserable lives. We strived for a real marriage, which was a struggle for us.

Having a big family was tough at times. And it was extremely tough to be in a blended family. I don't think either of us knew what we were getting into. I always imagined what a perfect relationship would look like, and then there was reality.

There were always outside voices and opinions. I mean it was always something. However we both made the best of it and made it happen.I was determined at having a successful relationship. All the other ones didn't mean much and ended on horrible terms. Leaving me feeling pitiful and full of shame and quilt. It left me wondering was I even worthy of a loving long-lasting relationship?

By now you should know how important family was to me. So it was a joy to get to know the moms of his other children. His son's mom Monica was very nice and had a warm spirit. I really liked her. One day I decided to surprise Royce by getting the kids and bringing them down to Tampa and I drove to Ocala to pick up Roy Roy.I was able to coordinate this by talking directly to his mom Monica. It was only his son this time because his daughter's mom Rhonda didn't like me from the jump. She always had a nasty attitude towards me and she didn't even know me. She hadn't even met me yet. However I understood how it is, when you have a bad breakup,feelings are still involved.

I know Royce and her were together for a little while and that he was once in love with this one. However the relationship didn't work because she constantly was cheating on him allegedly.. She had two other girls besides their daughter and because Royce and her were together. Those girls considered him to be their dad. Royce was definitely a good man with a big heart. He was the type of person that was portrayed to be hard, but behind all of that, he was a big soft teddy bear inside.

When we made it back to Tampa I never going to forget Royce walking in the door and walking in the living room to see Roy Roy sitting in the living room playing video games with the other kids. Roy Roy turned around and Royce ran to him to give him a big hug. The other kids ran to him as well. That night all you heard was loud voices and laughter. I loved that sound. Royce stayed up late with them. I stayed in the Bed, I always went to sleep early. I was sorta like a grandma in a young person's body.

For the next couple of years our lives consisted of just working and coming home and taking care of kids. Royce worked nights cleaning commercial buildings. I worked several different jobs over the years.

I just hated working for people and would quit and walk out of their offices in a minute. It was never an issue getting another Job ever however. So I think that's why I was never worried about leaving any employer. Furthermore something in me had a passion to work for myself I just didn't know how. I just remember whatever dream I had, Royce was there to support me every step of the way!

We didn't have much time for traveling or having lots of fun but when we did Royce would either travel to Ocala alone to see his family, and sometimes we would all go and just hang out and have fun. His mother Tasha was a very nice loving woman. She reminded me so much of my grandmother. We had such a beautiful relationship. I actually talked to her more than I talked to my own mother. She gave great advice. She never judged you, she was a great listener and she always encouraged you and believed in you. Her home was a home. It felt like a place you never wanted to leave.

This is how I felt when I was growing up with my grandmother. She was always so clean and the house was so fresh and you better believe she was always in the kitchen throwing down on a hot cooked meal. He also has a little sister on his moms side named Shaniya. She was fun to be around, and the kids love her as well. All you ever heard them say ws Tete Nay! Tete Nay! I felt loved and accepted in this family. Not only did they love my son I had with Royce but they loved and accepted all of the kids I had before him as well.

Rhonda, Aaliyah's mom finally came on board and dropped her attitude. She actually started talking to me and she decided to send aaliyah to live with us. I was happy that she was coming to live with us. Tiyrah would now have a sister to be with in the house that she could play with. It was tough being the only girl. Also Royce was able to see and be with all his kids at once without any drama. My kid's father was pretty much non-existent. They didn't talk to them, didn't call, didn't see them and the financial help was sporadic. You never knew when you would get support. So there wasn't drama from my end because it seemed as if they were dead.

Royce being the head of our household, he was also the disciplinary parent.I had one vision of raising kids and I had a different approach then he did. Sometimes our different views would clash and we would constantly be fighting and arguing. Royce and me both had tempers that were pretty outrageous so for us to be fighting it was always like world war two.

I was so used to being a single black independent woman and single mom, that I didn't know how to receive him, his help or his authority. I was accustomed to what already worked for me. We all know men and women are different anyway. But it was hard to relinquish that control over my life and my children. I didn't want anyone to hurt us so I was always on edge about all of our well beings.

At the time I didn't know that I was letting my kids get over on me, my kids were master manipulators and Royce was able to pinpoint it. I was in my "These my kids"era and never paid attention or listened to him. This was the downfall of our relationship. I wasn't allowing him to be a man. I was the man and the woman. He was just dealing with things he shouldn't have. The kids watched me go against the things he would say sometimes and that would in return have them losing respect for him.

He kept trying to show me things and tell me about the kids, sometimes it was a valid point and sometimes it wasn't. I think his delivery of what he was saying to me is why I wasn't receptive.In our household it was a lot of yelling ,cussing and just not hearing each other. It got to the point I would just walk off, and I think that made Royce even more angry. I think our relationship lacked intimacy, and not sex but love and being soft and sensual with each other. We rarely had alone time, we didn't hang out like that. It was boring to be honest. I was focused on raising the kids, so I would just let him hang out when he wanted to. I didn't have many friends and they didn't invite me to stuff like that because I never did anything.

The love we had for each other kept us together even on the bad days. Then creeps up 2018 and I'm now pregnant with my seventh child. I remember the night I conceived like it was yesterday because we didn't use protection and Royce was worried. I wanted to calm him down so I said don't worry if anything happens I will take care of it.I really didn't expect for me to get pregnant. Yes I was fertile but not that fast lol or so I thought. The smart thing to do was probably to do a plan B but I wasn't even thinking.

When I told Royce y'all know he went crazy. This would now be nine kids for us all together. How was I going to convince this man that we would be ok and would be able to take care of nine kids? I couldn't! And he was standing on business about what I said about taking care of it if something happened. Like literally.

I remember, when I told him he immediately said I wasn't keeping it. I remember calling the clinic and making an appointment. It was a gloomy Saturday morning. It was foggy but the air had a dry sting to it. We both drove to the university area in Tampa. It was a clinic Near Bruce B Downs & Fletcher that was behind the hospital. We pulled into the parking lot and we walked in the building. I immediately became full of anxiety from past memories of me having my last abortion began popping up in my brain.

In spite of all the fear in my heart, I walked to the counter and gave the receptionist my name. Royce walked over to the waiting area and took a seat. They showed me to the back. They took me to the sonogram room and advised the doctor would be in shortly. About ten minutes later she walks in. She asked how I was doing and I just shrugged my shoulders. So from there she didn't say much and quickly changed the subject.

"We are going to check and see how far along you are".She stated. Then asked me to remove my bottom half clothing and to place my legs up. I did as I was told. She inserted that little stick camera thing inside of me. She looked at the monitor as I did too. The first thing we both recognized was that the baby was moving around. It was so active. I was surprised. None of the babies I went to see this early moved around like this. The other funny thing was, I could feel the flutters too. Whooooh, how far along was I??

After doing some measurements, she wrote a few things on her notepad and then she told me I was around nine weeks old. I was always like nine or ten weeks everytime I found out I was pregnant. I put my clothes back on and the doctor said a lady would come in to get me to go over the next steps.

Soon a blonde short lady walked in and asked me to follow her. We walked across the hall to an office. It was a small office but it was warm and welcoming. She had candles lit that left an apple cider aroma. Her curtains were of a rustic orange and brownish color. She had pictures of her family up on the walls. Also pictures of a big fluffy dog was on top of her desk.

She took a seat and asked was this my decision to have an abortion today. I looked at her and said no. She marked my answer down on her notepad. Then she followed by asking "Was I 100% sure I wanted to do this today"?

I answered that question as a "No"as well. She placed her pen down on the desk and she removed her glasses from off of her face. She looked directly at me and with her soft spoken voice she proceeded to say I wouldn't be able to do the procedure because for one it wasn't my decision and furthermore, I was not 100% sure about the procedure anyway.

The counselor expounded on what she was saying and then asked me how I felt.I broke down in tears right in front of her. In the middle of my tears I was able to say that my boyfriend was in the office and he really wanted me to do this but I didn't want to.

I was so emotional and crying hysterically at this point. The counselor grabbed a handful of tissues and walked over to me and handed me the tissue.

She then gave me the biggest hug. Oh boy did I need this hug. I didn't have anyone to ask me how I was doing in such a long time. I was the go-to person to person for everyone. I was the one checking on everyone and no one was checking on me. It felt good that a person actually cared at that moment. After I pulled myself together.

The counselor came up with a great idea. She lit up with excitement and said "Hey! I can help you Ashley! You are my priority. I am going to get you out of here safely.She said that she was going to say we are unable to complete the procedure today due to my blood pressure being way too high. She also suggested giving me at least three days to sit on this decision and if I really wanted to do this after, then I was indeed able to visit the clinic and complete the procedure.

She gave me a final hug and then grabbed my hand to get up. She walked me to the door with her clipboard. We both walked to the door that would lead me to the lobby. I knew Royce was on the other side of the door, and I was trying to prepare for what was to come once this lady dropped the bad news that the procedure would not happen today.

As we opened the door, she called Royce over and she pointed to her clipboard and stated that at this time, the procedure couldn't be completed because my blood pressure was too high at this time. She was also informed of rescheduling and coming back in three days.If looks could kill then Royce would have killed us all.He left and walked to the car, as the counselor walked me to the front. She gave me a partial refund. I still had to pay for the sonogram but the rest of the money was given back to me.

After gaining my refund and receipt, I walked outside and got in the car. I literally walked into Royce's tornado.

"I knew you shouldn't have eaten those salty fries on the way here, That's why your blood pressure was so high! Now we have to wait three days to come back. So make sure you call to schedule another appointment! He screamed.

I sat there driving feeling numb. I didn't respond back or say a word to him. There was nothing that I needed to say. I was keeping my baby and that was that! When we got home with the other kids I made sure to start fixing them something to eat. Royce was walking around with an attitude as usual and wasn't speaking to me.

He didn't speak to me for four months following us leaving the abortion clinic.After that day I never called the clinic and I never said anything else to him about an abortion. I just wasn't going to do it and if he wanted to leave me because of my decision I was already prepared for him to do so.

Royce would only talk to me through the kids, he would send either one of them to ask me things he wanted to know or to give me information.He gave me the silent treatment for the longest time. The kids would come up to me saying "Daddy said what are we eating tonight? "Daddy said is he picking up the boys from school"

I got so sick of him talking through them, I sent them back to him and demanded them to tell him"TELL YOUR DADDY HE CAN COME TO

TALK TO ME!"

Which he didn't. He didn't start talking to me until around the time when we found out it was another boy.I was kinda disappointed because I wanted it to be a girl so bad. We already had so many boys. However the most important thing was just to give birth to a healthy baby.

Since we were expecting another baby soon, Royce and I started working on getting a bigger place. At this time we were living in a four bedroom apartment that we truly had outgrown. There was limited space for the kids to run and play and just relax.Thankfully we both found a six bedroom 3200 sq foot home in Riverview.Once we were approved we moved right on in and surprised the kids of the new place.

I was so happy we did, because I gave birth to our last baby boy Tameer in November.He was such a healthy baby, but I was the most depressed that I had ever been in life after having him. I loved him but I felt like he deserved a different mom. I felt less than a woman and just was down right broken.No one knew what I was going through, not even Royce.I kept it all to myself.

The only thing that I indeed got help with was putting Tameer to sleep. My second oldest TJ was who I called the baby whisperer. He was able to calm Tameer and also put him to sRoycep in just a matter of seconds.The baby just loved him. No matter what I did, it just seemed Tameer wasn't relaxed. All he did was squirm and move around and look everywhere. I was sleep deprived and I felt I just wasn't getting enough rest. I would find myself waking up in the middle of the night and forgetting that the baby was with TJ.

I would run to his room in panic, and I would walk into the most beautiful kodak moment. Tj was knocked out with his mouth open and Tameer was in a little dog pale with blood so no one would roll on him, fast asleep on his back. I would grab the pale then place it in my bed and go back to sleep while he was still sRoyceping.

Right now I would say Life was o.k, it wasn't great, but we were blessed. We had come a long way and I was just so proud of Royce for how hard we both worked to give our kids a home that we both never had growing up.

James 1:2 Blessed is the man who remains steadfast under trial, for when he has stood the test, he will receive the crown of life, which God has promised to those who love him.

I was sort of a secret to everyone with Royce. He was very private when it came to his personal life. I had held a secret about my being pregnant for as long as I could. I was around eight months, and now everyone knew I was pregnant again with my sixth child. I was so happy the cat was out of the bag. I was sick of keeping it to myself.

In August, I gave birth to our Son Trevian. He was such a beautiful chocolate baby boy, too. I was so happy to hold him in my arms. Despite all the junk Royce talked about before our son was born, you saw how he melted when he was holding him as well.

I must admit our relationship was sped up, and it kind of happened so fast I felt like I didn't have any control over it. We soon moved together, and one thing about me was that I was a woman who made sure men were in their children's lives. So Royce had two other children outside of me from two different women.

He grew up in a small country city called Ocala, so the kids and their moms lived there. His oldest was his son, Roy Roy, and his daughter, Aaliyah. When I met them, Roy Roy was five, and Aaliyah was three years old. It was a joy to have all of the kids around each other. They all got along most of the time, and when I tell you, our house was never a dull moment.

Royce & I were raising them the best way we knew how. We didn't have anyone to look up to for guidance. No one in either of our families was married with the amount of children that we had. Also, even if they were married, we didn't know how to decipher them having a healthy, stable marriage. It was a lot of cover-ups, secrets, lies, and deception. Marriage didn't seem like something that people took seriously. They would only count the number of years they were together as success but were really living miserable lives. We strived for a real marriage, which was a struggle for us.

Having a big family was tough at times. And it was extremely tough to be in a blended family. I don't think either of us knew what we were getting into. I always imagined what a perfect relationship would look like, and then there was reality.

There were always outside voices and opinions. I mean it was always something. However we both made the best of it and made it happen.I was determined at having a successful relationship. All the other ones didn't mean much and ended on horrible terms. Leaving me feeling pitiful and full of shame and quilt. It left me wondering was I even worthy of a loving long-lasting relationship?

By now you should know how important family was to me. So it was a joy to get to know the moms of his other children. His son's mom Monica was very nice and had a warm spirit. I really liked her. One day I decided to surprise Royce by getting the kids and bringing them down to Tampa and I drove to Ocala to pick up Roy Roy. I was able to coordinate this by talking directly to his mom Monica. It was only his son this time because his daughter's mom Rhonda didn't like me from the jump. She always had a nasty attitude towards me and she didn't even know me. She hadn't even met me yet. However I understood how it is, when you have a bad breakup, feelings are still involved.

I know Royce and her were together for a little while and that he was once in love with this one. However the relationship didn't work because she constantly was cheating on him allegedly.. She had two other girls besides their daughter and because Royce and her were together. Those girls considered him to be their dad. Royce was definitely a good man with a big heart. He was the type of person that was portrayed to be hard, but behind all of that, he was a big soft teddy bear inside.

When we made it back to Tampa I never going to forget Royce walking in the door and walking in the living room to see Roy Roy sitting in the living room playing video games with the other kids. Roy Roy turned around and Royce ran to him to give him a big hug. The other kids ran to him as well. That night all you heard was loud voices and laughter. I loved that sound. Royce stayed up late with them. I stayed in the Bed, I always went to sleep early. I was sorta like a grandma in a young person's body.

For the next couple of years our lives consisted of just working and coming home and taking care of kids. Royce worked nights cleaning commercial buildings. I worked several different jobs over the years.

I just hated working for people and would quit and walk out of their offices in a minute. It was never an issue getting another Job ever however. So I think that's why I was never worried about leaving any employer. Furthermore something in me had a passion to work for myself I just didn't know how. I just remember whatever dream I had, Royce was there to support me every step of the way!

We didn't have much time for traveling or having lots of fun but when we did Royce would either travel to Ocala alone to see his family, and sometimes we would all go and just hang out and have fun. His mother Tasha was a very nice loving woman. She reminded me so much of my grandmother. We had such a beautiful relationship. I actually talked to her more than I talked to my own mother. She gave great advice. She never judged you, she was a great listener and she always encouraged you and believed in you. Her home was a home. It felt like a place you never wanted to leave.

This is how I felt when I was growing up with my grandmother. She was always so clean and the house was so fresh and you better believe she was always in the kitchen throwing down on a hot cooked meal. He also has a little sister on his moms side named Shaniya. She was fun to be around, and the kids love her as well. All you ever heard them say ws Tete Nay! Tete Nay! I felt loved and accepted in this family. Not only did they love my son I had with Royce but they loved and accepted all of the kids I had before him as well.

Rhonda, Aaliyah's mom finally came on board and dropped her attitude. She actually started talking to me and she decided to send aaliyah to live with us. I was happy that she was coming to live with us. Tiyrah would now have a sister to be with in the house that she could play with. It was tough being the only girl. Also Royce was able to see and be with all his kids at once without any drama. My kid's father was pretty much non-existent. They didn't talk to them, didn't call, didn't see them and the financial help was sporadic. You never knew when you would get support. So there wasn't drama from my end because it seemed as if they were dead.

Royce being the head of our household, he was also the disciplinary parent.I had one vision of raising kids and I had a different approach then he did. Sometimes our different views would clash and we would constantly be fighting and arguing. Royce and me both had tempers that were pretty outrageous so for us to be fighting it was always like world war two.

I was so used to being a single black independent woman and single mom, that I didn't know how to receive him, his help or his authority. I was accustomed to what already worked for me. We all know men and women are different anyway. But it was hard to relinquish that control over my life and my children. I didn't want anyone to hurt us so I was always on edge about all of our well beings.

At the time I didn't know that I was letting my kids get over on me, my kids were master manipulators and Royce was able to pinpoint it. I was in my "These my kids"era and never paid attention or listened to him. This was the downfall of our relationship. I wasn't allowing him to be a man. I was the man and the woman. He was just dealing with things he shouldn't have. The kids watched me go against the things he would say sometimes and that would in return have them losing respect for him.

He kept trying to show me things and tell me about the kids, sometimes it was a valid point and sometimes it wasn't. I think his delivery of what he was saying to me is why I wasn't receptive.In our household it was a lot of yelling ,cussing and just not hearing each other. It got to the point I would just walk off, and I think that made Royce even more angry. I think our relationship lacked intimacy, and not sex but love and being soft and sensual with each other. We rarely had alone time, we didn't hang out like that. It was boring to be honest. I was focused on raising the kids, so I would just let him hang out when he wanted to. I didn't have many friends and they didn't invite me to stuff like that because I never did anything.

The love we had for each other kept us together even on the bad days. Then creeps up 2018 and I'm now pregnant with my seventh child. I remember the night I conceived like it was yesterday because we didn't use protection and Royce was worried. I wanted to calm him down so I said don't worry if anything happens I will take care of it.I really didn't expect for me to get pregnant. Yes I was fertile but not that fast lol or so I thought. The smart thing to do was probably to do a plan B but I wasn't even thinking.

When I told Royce y'all know he went crazy. This would now be nine kids for us all together. How was I going to convince this man that we would be ok and would be able to take care of nine kids? I couldn't! And he was standing on business about what I said about taking care of it if something happened. Like literally.

I remember, when I told him he immediately said I wasn't keeping it. I remember calling the clinic and making an appointment. It was a gloomy Saturday morning. It was foggy but the air had a dry sting to it. We both drove to the university area in Tampa. It was a clinic Near Bruce B Downs & Fletcher that was behind the hospital. We pulled into the parking lot and we walked in the building. I immediately became full of anxiety from past memories of me having my last abortion began popping up in my brain.

In spite of all the fear in my heart, I walked to the counter and gave the receptionist my name. Royce walked over to the waiting area and took a seat. They showed me to the back. They took me to the sonogram room and advised the doctor would be in shortly. About ten minutes later she walks in. She asked how I was doing and I just shrugged my shoulders. So from there she didn't say much and quickly changed the subject.

"We are going to check and see how far along you are".She stated. Then asked me to remove my bottom half clothing and to place my legs up. I did as I was told. She inserted that little stick camera thing inside of me. She looked at the monitor as I did too. The first thing we both recognized was that the baby was moving around. It was so active. I was surprised. None of the babies I went to see this early moved around like this. The other funny thing was, I could feel the flutters too. Whooooh, how far along was I??

After doing some measurements, she wrote a few things on her notepad and then she told me I was around nine weeks old. I was always like nine or ten weeks everytime I found out I was pregnant. I put my clothes back on and the doctor said a lady would come in to get me to go over the next steps.

Soon a blonde short lady walked in and asked me to follow her. We walked across the hall to an office. It was a small office but it was warm and welcoming. She had candles lit that left an apple cider aroma. Her curtains were of a rustic orange and brownish color. She had pictures of her family up on the walls. Also pictures of a big fluffy dog was on top of her desk.

She took a seat and asked was this my decision to have an abortion today. I looked at her and said no. She marked my answer down on her notepad. Then she followed by asking "Was I 100% sure I wanted to do this today"?

I answered that question as a "No"as well. She placed her pen down on the desk and she removed her glasses from off of her face. She looked directly at me and with her soft spoken voice she proceeded to say I wouldn't be able to do the procedure because for one it wasn't my decision and furthermore, I was not 100% sure about the procedure anyway.

The counselor expounded on what she was saying and then asked me how I felt.I broke down in tears right in front of her. In the middle of my tears I was able to say that my boyfriend was in the office and he really wanted me to do this but I didn't want to.

I was so emotional and crying hysterically at this point. The counselor grabbed a handful of tissues and walked over to me and handed me the tissue.

She then gave me the biggest hug. Oh boy did I need this hug. I didn't have anyone to ask me how I was doing in such a long time. I was the go-to person to person for everyone. I was the one checking on everyone and no one was checking on me. It felt good that a person actually cared at that moment. After I pulled myself together.

The counselor came up with a great idea. She lit up with excitement and said "Hey! I can help you Ashley! You are my priority. I am going to get you out of here safely.She said that she was going to say we are unable to complete the procedure today due to my blood pressure being way too high. She also suggested giving me at least three days to sit on this decision and if I really wanted to do this after, then I was indeed able to visit the clinic and complete the procedure.

She gave me a final hug and then grabbed my hand to get up. She walked me to the door with her clipboard. We both walked to the door that would lead me to the lobby. I knew Royce was on the other side of the door, and I was trying to prepare for what was to come once this lady dropped the bad news that the procedure would not happen today.

As we opened the door, she called Royce over and she pointed to her clipboard and stated that at this time, the procedure couldn't be completed because my blood pressure was too high at this time. She was also informed of rescheduling and coming back in three days.If looks could kill then Royce would have killed us all.He left and walked to the car, as the counselor walked me to the front. She gave me a partial refund. I still had to pay for the sonogram but the rest of the money was given back to me.

After gaining my refund and receipt, I walked outside and got in the car. I literally walked into Royce's tornado.

"I knew you shouldn't have eaten those salty fries on the way here, That's why your blood pressure was so high! Now we have to wait three days to come back. So make sure you call to schedule another appointment! He screamed.

I sat there driving feeling numb. I didn't respond back or say a word to him. There was nothing that I needed to say. I was keeping my baby and that was that! When we got home with the other kids I made sure to start fixing them something to eat. Royce was walking around with an attitude as usual and wasn't speaking to me.

He didn't speak to me for four months following us leaving the abortion clinic.After that day I never called the clinic and I never said anything else to him about an abortion. I just wasn't going to do it and if he wanted to leave me because of my decision I was already prepared for him to do so.

Royce would only talk to me through the kids, he would send either one of them to ask me things he wanted to know or to give me information.He gave me the silent treatment for the longest time. The kids would come up to me saying "Daddy said what are we eating tonight? "Daddy said is he picking up the boys from school"

I got so sick of him talking through them, I sent them back to him and demanded them to tell him"TELL YOUR DADDY HE CAN COME TO TALK TO ME "!

Which he didn't. He didn't start talking to me until around the time when we found out it was another boy.I was kinda disappointed because I wanted it to be a girl so bad. We already had so many boys. However the most important thing was just to give birth to a healthy baby.

Since we were expecting another baby soon, Royce and I started working on getting a bigger place. At this time we were living in a four bedroom apartment that we truly had outgrown. There was limited space for the kids to run and play and just relax.Thankfully we both found a six bedroom 3200 sq foot home in Riverview.Once we were approved we moved right on in and surprised the kids of the new place.

I was so happy we did, because I gave birth to our last baby boy Tameer in November.He was such a healthy baby, but I was the most depressed that I had ever been in life after having him. I loved him but I felt like he deserved a different mom. I felt less than a woman and just was down right broken.No one knew what I was going through, not even Royce.I kept it all to myself.

The only thing that I indeed got help with was putting Tameer to sleep. My second oldest TJ was who I called the baby whisperer. He was able to calm Tameer and also put him to sRoycep in just a matter of seconds.The baby just loved him. No matter what I did, it just seemed Tameer wasn't relaxed. All he did was squirm and move around and look everywhere. I was sleep deprived and I felt I just wasn't getting enough rest. I would find myself waking up in the middle of the night and forgetting that the baby was with TJ.

I would run to his room in panic, and I would walk into the most beautiful kodak moment. Tj was knocked out with his mouth open and Tameer was in a little dog pale with blood so no one would roll on him, fast asleep on his back. I would grab the pale then place it in my bed and go back to sleep while he was still sRoyceping.

Right now I would say Life was o.k, it wasn't great, but we were blessed. We had come a long way and I was just so proud of Royce for how hard we both worked to give our kids a home that we both never had growing up.

James 1:2 Blessed is the man who remains steadfast under trial, for when he has stood the test, he will receive the crown of life, which God has promised to those who love him.

CHAPTER 28: COVID-19 CHANGED OUR LIVES

By now and I Royce had been together for almost five years, and the family on each side began to pressure us about being married. My biological father, whom I always called PAPA, confronted Royce about marrying me. I'm not sure how that conversation went. I just remember my mom doing the same thing.

 She would comment that "we were together this long and shacking up, and that we might go ahead and get married"!.

Everyone was in our ears. I wish we didn't have all these voices in our ears to force us to make such an important decision like that. His mother, Tasha, would even throw different hints at me about being married. Since all of these people were sharing their opinions, it made me feel less than.

 Then I started to ask myself. "Hmmm, why didn't he ask to marry me yet"?

No one took the time to sit us down and ask how we felt about marriage. The hardest thing was that we didn't see a successful marriage, which seemed impossible.

On the flip side, I just decided to make it happen. I was tired of everyone knowing me as ASHLEY WITH ALL THE KIDS!!! He just lay up with me all these years and reaped benefits, and I wasn't his wife. I cut myself short, and I also robbed him of something beautiful for him to ask for my hand in marriage. There was no proposal. There was no surprise there was nothing! I can't even remember how the conversation went, but we only mentioned it.

The next thing you know, I was planning a wedding we couldn't afford!

As I mentioned my concerns about the affordability of a wedding, his mom suggested we just go to a park and then plan for our big wedding on a different date. I went for that, and I chose the University of Tampa Park. Everything concerning this marriage was forced and expedited.

I bought a white beautiful low-back wedding gown from the marketplace .However the morning of our wedding day my cycle came on. So I had to quickly switch to wearing a red dress. Royce bought a white dress shirt, white pants and red bow tie and red shoes. The older boys wore Red polo shirts and black shorts

149

The little boys wore blue jean like shirts and red shorts. The girls wore white dresses with red and blue stripes. We all were presentable. However this was not the vision for my wedding day.

The only family members that were there for me were my brother Reishard, My uncle Pat and my aunt Terri. My Godmother Tami and my oldest God sister Shauny also showed up. Royce had all of his parents there. His mom, step dad, his step mom and father, his little sister and one of the twins Antonetta.

It was really intimate.A church mother married us. I would call her ma, she reminded me so much of my granny. Just an old school older lady who loved the Lord but didn't play the radio.We did our marriage counseling with her but we didn't do the normal amount of sessions someone would usually do. Due to the timeframe of getting married, we only had one session with her.

There were so many red flags before walking to the altar and saying I-Do to my husband. However, we both ignored them all and we both said I-Do on July 13, 2019. I really loved my husband and I was a bit excited that I was now a wife. I couldn't help but think about how my papa wasn't there to walk me down the aisle(I mean it was really concrete, but you know what I mean lol) and my mother wasn't even there. The crazy thing about that, we changed our original date, so my mother and her husband could make it and they still didn't show.

After the wedding, we all attempted to eat at a place like Kobe's Steakhouse, but it was called Koizi's. They served the same hibachi food however, it was all you can eat. The way was so long, and we were starving from hunger, we settled to go to Steak & shake right across the street instead.

I'm not going to lie. I was still happy that we were all together, and all we did was laugh, talk, and enjoy each other's company. Today was actually a good day, in spite of not being my actual dream.

Now we were the HICKS, with nine children. Seven boys and two girls. There was no one that had the family dynamics that we had. No one could even give us advice. We received more support from Royce's family than mine. Once my granny died, my kids didn't really have a real grandma. My mom didn't come and get them or spend time with them often. It was always sporadic and for short moments at a time. Times like this are when I really miss my granny. I wish she were here with us now

After having a new baby in the house and now being married, adapting to that change with seven other kids in the house, we then had to adapt to a change no one in the world was ready for. Covid virus began to spread throughout the nation and all schools and some jobs were shut down. Everyone was sent home to work and complete school from home.

Royce's son Roy came to our house and stayed with us the time we were on lock down for covid. It definitely was around five or so months.Royce and I were surrounded by nine kids ALL DAY EVERYDAY. The youngest was a baby and our oldest Tiyrel was just a freshman in highschool.This mentally drained the both of us.I didn't know this then but we actually both fell into a depression state. Our circumstances and way of living had drastically changed.

We nearly had every age group and classroom in our house.Starting at headstart all the way to highschool. This is where we were challenged if we were smarter than second graders, third graders and middle schoolers. I really couldn't remember doing any of this work those kids start showing us.We all were just stuck in the house and I think that was driving all of us crazy. I knew for a fact Royce was down and depressed and didn't want to verbalize it.

When covid hit, a lot of the buildings he was cleaning no longer needed services because they had sent everyone home to work. So janitorial services were now shut down until further notice with a lot of companies.When this happened you could see the shift in Royce's well being. He became down,sad, sluggish, lazy and slothful. It was like he had zero motivation to get himself up.I was used to this man being a hard worker,self determined and all.That man would work, you hear me ?

When I noticed his behavior I immediately started applying for Jobs. I saw him struggling and didn't want him to drown. He didn't ask me to go back to work and he didn't have to. I wasn't a lazy woman and I've always worked. It was nothing for me to go and get a job. Just like that I started working for a medical company about two weeks from then.Everything was ok but just for that moment.

However, I was driving all the way to Tampa for work and we lived in Riverview. The commute there and back took almost two hours because of all the traffic. I wouldn't get home until after 7pm on some days.I was often tired and burned out. I must say me and Royce were a team. He would already be cooking or have fed the kids. When I walked in the door I literally could just shower, talk to everybody for a bit and head to bed after I got everyone baths and settled in.As a father he was doing amazing Job and making sure I could relax coming home.

That just left me and baby Tameer to get to bed, as soon as he was asleep, I was able to do the same. We had the same routine like clock work in our home. Once everyone was off to bed. Royce was able to head out to work to do the building he had to complete by morning. I slept in the bed just for myself for years and then of course whenever the kids would join me. But he wouldn't want to wake us up when he came in, so he just stayed downstairs for the most part.

Royce & I didn't have a lot of "US TIME ". We were never really away from the kids. Especially me. At Least he was able to hang out over my Uncle pats and get a break from the house, or his other friends. I didn't do anything or go anywhere at all.This really affected our relationship. There was no intimacy or times we really could just enjoy each other and not with kids.We were just parents who paid the bills and took care of the children.This was a major Shift for Royce because when I met him all he did was hang-out and party. Now he was a family Guy. He changed for us.

Then there was the stress of finances, when you have a big family as big as ours the cost of living is magnified by the additional heads and mouths you have to provide for. Since it was still the year of covid work didn't pick up for Royce. I noticed he would leave the house, not giving me any details about his whereabouts, he would stay out like he was on his work shift. He would come into the house around four or five in the morning.

I remember this particular night, I heard his car pull up and his bright headlight brightened up the driveway. Our room was upstairs and towards the front of the home, so I jumped out of bed and peeked through the window.I saw him getting out of the car and walking into the garage. Once he made it inside the house I walked over to grab my robe from off the bathroom door. I proceed downstairs to meet him.

I made it downstairs and met him in the kitchen, he was pouring himself something to drink. His back was turned towards me.

Then I asked "So where have you been all night"?

"Bruh don't ask me no questions man"! He replied I hated when Royce called me bruh he had no respect for me as his wife. He just talked to me as if I was one of his homeboys or something.We had an argument that had been festering over for awhile now and Royce still had an attitude towards me.All of our altercations normally included the kids.It was rare that we were mad at eachother for something him & I did to one another.

The kids were the main reason we were always fighting.For one kids play both sides, they also are mass manipulators and liars. They will do anything to get their way. It's hard having a blended family and also having a blended family and not being equipped with what it takes for it to run smoothly. You definitely have to create boundaries with your kids and your spouse. Those kids can not Run you!

One night when Royce was working, I gathered all the kids together as I normally did. I loved spending time with all of them.I enjoyed getting to know them.We would talk, laugh and play games etc. Our big family was a safe haven for me.So they all gathered in my room and I would just do check-ins to see how they felt and to see what me and Royce could do in order to be better parents or to make their lives more peaceful or happier.

Some of them would share their thoughts while others had nothing to say and mentioned everything was fine.It was now Roy's turn and he mentioned what was on his heart. Then out of nowhere his little sister Aaliyah responded not having any compassion and her response made him cry.

I got onto aaliyah and told her she was wrong, but I also addressed Roy's concern. Him and TJ were the boys that didn't speak their minds, they kept everything inside so if they did speak you better make it your business to listen.

He was ok for the rest of the night and they went off to play games.Aaliyah apologized to her brother and everything was fine. Royce however was told that I was the one that made Roy cry and Royce made it his business to let me know he didn't appreciate that.

 I asked where he got that information ,and he said Roy told him and a few other kids without names.This angered me.The kids couldn't have told him this. Everyone was in the room when his sister clearly made him cry. This was a lie. I would never hurt a child intentionally. And if I did I would apologize and fix it. Royce held onto this for a good while, I knew he was still upset.

This explained the attitude I was still getting from Royce in the kitchen.
"I'm your wife, and I can ask you where you've been, what do you mean"?

When I looked Royce in his eyes, they were bloodshot red. But he didn't look at himself, It was like I was conversing with an actual Demon.

He just laughed and really was not stunting what I was saying. His body language and him ignoring me was really aggravating me. So I begin to say you out all night while I'm stuck in this house with these kids. I'm tired from working all the time and pay bills!........

Then he blurts out "I PAY BILL IN THIS BIT*** too!!!"he screamed

Now Royce definitely was a great provider post Covid. I never had to worry about me and the kids having anything. He would make it work. That's what I loved about him. A lot of people and their income and financial status changes once covid hits. But remember he had become complacent. At that moment I had taken care of everything for that month and didn't ask him for anything. So my comeback was:

"What bills you paid"!!!!?? I paid all the bills this month! We began to go back and forth and every time each of us said something it was getting more and more heated.Royce knew how to get under my skin and I knew what buttons to press with him as well. When we would argue it was a case of who can go below the belt more!

The next thing that comes out of his mouth is that he didn't ask for my kids that I had with him to be here. He said Trevian wasn't supposed to be here and then he said our youngest Tameer wasn't supposed to be here either.

This isn't the first time that Royce had brought this up or even mentioned this to me. I was sick of him saying my kids are not supposed to be here.

I do understand our kids were not brought into the world because we planned them, but they were here now. Those boys loved Royce to the moon!

"So if my kids aren't supposed to be here,why won't you kill Roy , he is not supposed to be here either, right"?!!

I knew this had Royce boiling inside from my comment. His eyes were bloodshot red.The way he looked at me was so evil.I felt he was going to hurt me. I ran away up the stairs to get away from him but I'm heading to the boys room where they are asleep. I woke up Roy and I told him to pack up his stuff and to call his mom to come pick him up.

He was like half asleep so I don't even know if what I was saying registered to him.He wanted to lie to Royce and say that I made him cry and I was sick of these kids causing chaos. My kids had done the same thing a couple times with Royce. They would just make up lies, and then drama was created and he and the adults were left fighting over it.

One thing I learned is that you and your husband have to be on the same page when it comes to your kids.Do-Not let them play you against each other.

Royce had finally made it upstairs and was screaming and yelling at me in my face. At this point both of us were screaming at each other at the top of our lungs. I'm sure the kids were all woken up by our big mouths and aggressive behavior.It was really bad.I hated the kids having to witness or experience this from us.

Royce must have contacted Roy's mom because his mom came and got him that night a few hours later. I just wanted Royce far away from me! I told him to get out. The next morning, he packed Aaliyah and all his stuff up while I was at work, and he drove both of them to Ocala.This was June 26, 2020. Once he left us on that day, he had never come back.

My heart was hurting so bad. I knew we had just had a bad argument, but now my family was falling apart. I tried calling Royce back to back, and he wouldn't answer the phone. I only knew Aaliyah was gone as well because the kids told me he took her. I hated that he took her because she was in a stable home. She was doing so well in school, and I didn't want her to go back to an environment that wasn't going to allow her to excel.

A couple months had then passed .I found myself begging Royce to come home so we could work on our marriage. We even had all the kids in Orlando as we rented an AirBnb for Trevians birthday. He never listened and he never came home. So I just conformed to my reality of being yet another single mother. Now I was just a married single mother. There were several times me and Royce would talk about the future, we would meet up in Tampa or Ocala. We would hang out with the kids etc. It was just not enough to fix all of our issues.

He felt unheard, I felt unheard. He felt disrespected, I felt disrespected. It was this constant battle that seemed like it never would be resolved no matter what we did. I constantly prayed and I asked God that if Royce was the man for me, then bring him home. Royce never came home. I don't know what was keeping him in his hometown. I didn't know how long this would last.

He wanted us to move there, and I considered it, making plans, but deep down, I couldn't find peace with the idea. Ocala held nothing for us, and this caused tension between Royce and me.

As over three years passed, the strain of living apart grew unbearable. I didn't want to argue anymore or explain myself. All I craved was peace and what was best for both of us.

So, I made the tough choice to file for divorce. On October 6, 2023, I started the process, and by December 20, 2023, it was finalized. I thought I'd feel relief, but instead, I felt sadness and shock. Being with him since 2014, being his wife— it was all over.

But I needed to prioritize loving myself over him. I knew my worth and refused to stay in an unhealthy relationship, living by others' expectations. It was time to draw closer to God, rediscover myself, and embrace my femininity. I wanted to shed the controlling habits learned from the dominant women in my life, reclaiming my true self.

As I gazed into the mirror, my prayer was simple: that God would align every part of me with His word. I pledged to live righteously and walk in my purpose, obedient to God's will. This prayer extended to my husband, knowing he too had a divine calling.

Despite my struggles, mistakes, and trials, God used every bit for His glory. I realized that sharing our imperfections and past stories, despite fear of judgment, reveals God's power and grace.

I was determined to share my story authentically, straight from the source. Nothing compares to speaking truth firsthand.

 I've been through it all—abandonment issues from my father, mommy and daddy issues, becoming a teen mom at fourteen, neglecting my body as a temple, raising seven children with different fathers, getting arrested, being coerced into things I didn't want to do, having a selfish attitude, enduring a divorce, and struggling to understand my own worth.

But despite all of that, God still chose me!

Jesus said he was rewriting my story—what was their tea, became my testimony! I've been set free.

Let me reintroduce myself.

I'm Ashley Hicks, the beacon for young girls labeled as troubled, offering the love, support, and guidance they need to overcome challenges.

I empower teen moms to navigate the complexities of early motherhood, helping them face the challenges of being both a new parent and a teenager.

With a steadfast heart, I support single mothers, guiding them through the journey of raising their children solo.

As a fierce advocate, I champion the resilience and strength of survivors of human trafficking and sexual assault.

Standing alongside women navigating the storms of divorce, I offer unwavering support and the assurance that there is life and hope after divorce.

I am CALLED! And I AM CHOSEN!

Today, I'm a Best Selling published author, motivational speaker, certified life coach, and parenting coach. I specialize in helping at-risk youth, teen moms, and single mothers heal from their past traumas so they can embrace their God-given purpose.

But you know what's even more remarkable?

It took every hardship I faced to finally claim the promise. If you're feeling unworthy, burdened by your past mistakes, or convinced you'll never amount to anything—those are all lies from the enemy! Forgive yourself and those who've hurt you. No matter what's happened, remember you are God's precious jewel.

In Corinthians 1:27, God reveals He chooses imperfect people to fulfill His purpose. Everything is for His glory! God isn't concerned with your flaws; He wants you raw and real so that when He transforms you, everyone will witness His power and be amazed—it's all God's doing!

Always Remember YOU ARE ENOUGH, there is NOTHING too big for GOD & you were FEARFULLY & WONDERFULLY MADE.

So hold your head up, Fix your crown and walk in your Purpose!!

THIS IS YOUR REBIRTH!! You will conquer after every trial and claim the promise meant for you. I love you from the bottom of my heart! I can't wait to hear your Testimony!

Love,

Coach Ashley Hicks

ABOUT THE AUTHOR

Ashley Hicks is not just a Mother of Multiples; she is a beacon of strength, a compassionate friend, sister, coach, and mentor to many. As a Transformational Life Coach, Ashley draws from her own life experiences to guide girls, teens, and women worldwide through healing from past traumas, empowering them to embrace their divine purpose.

A proud and resilient Black woman, Ashley courageously shares her insecurities to assure other women that they are not alone on their healing journey. Her mission is to heal the world, one person at a time. When you meet Coach Ashley, you encounter a heavenly angel ready to walk beside you, imparting essential life skills to overcome adversity and thrive.

Email: Coaching@ashs2beauty.com
Social Media:
Facebook: Author Ashley Hicks
Instagram:Coachashleyhicks
Tiktok:Coachashleyhicks
Website:www.ashs2beauty.com (for Speaking engagements/ Bookings)

Made in the USA
Columbia, SC
13 October 2024

43511160R10095